The Winemaker's Guide

Essential Information for Making Wine and Champagne
Revised Edition

by
F. S. Nury, Ph.D.
Professor of Enology and Food Science
California State University, Fresno, California

K. C. Fugelsang, M.A.
Enologist-Food Scientist
California State University, Fresno, California

WESTERN TANAGER PRESS
SANTA CRUZ

Western Tanager Press
1111 Pacific Avenue
Santa Cruz, CA 95060
Cover by Linda Knudson

Library of Congress Catalog Number 78-65264
ISBN 0-934136-27-0

Contents

INTRODUCTION

Wine has been the drink of man for thousands of years. In Genesis 9:20-21, Noah is credited with the first production of grapes and consumption of wine. Technology of production and storage of wine has improved dramatically over the several thousand years since Noah lived. An ever-increasing emphasis on wine consumption in the United States has led to the growth of the interesting and educational hobby of home winemaking. The rapid growth of home wine-making in the past several years should not be considered as an alternative to the purchase of the many high quality commercial products, but rather as a desire to explore the process and to produce a wine that, in the opinion of the winemaker, "could rival its commercial counterpart." This book is presented to aid the amateur winemaker in producing such a wine. However, the information presented can be helpful to all winemakers and wine connoisseurs as well.

1

EQUIPMENT AND SUPPLIES FOR PRODUCTION OF WINE

WITH DEVELOPMENT in technology has come the necessary task of enforcement of standards and practices. The Federal governmental agency which regulates the wine industry is the Bureau of Alcohol, Tobacco and Firearms, within the Department of Treasury. According to law, a head of household may produce up to 200 gallons of wine per year for consumption on his premises, but not before filing government permit number 1541, which may be obtained at your local BATF office. Governmental interpretation of "head of household" is any member over the age of 21 who has filed a tax return during the current year. There is no restriction as to sex, but this does not mean that if husband and wife file separate returns their total production for the year can be increased to 400 gallons.

Once the necessary permit has been secured, the first consideration of the home winemaker should be the equipment needed to produce an acceptable product. The following list is provided as a guide:

      Crusher-stemmer
      Press
      Fermentation and storage containers
      Transfer hoses
      Filters
      Bottles and corks
      Miscellaneous supplies

In a large-scale industrial operation, these items could easily cost in excess of a million dollars. However, with the following suggestions, one should be able to furnish a home winery for less than $100.

Crusher-stemmer

The purpose of this piece of equipment is to achieve rupture of berries and removal of stems and leaves. Crusher-stemmers scaled to small lot production are available, but are relatively expensive. Prices range from $200 to $1,000, depending upon capacity and mode of power. Although occasionally one may rent this equipment at wine supply outlets, a workable alternative is the time-honored method of crushing by foot. The necessary stem and leaf removal is then effected by hand. While this method is lengthy, as compared with a crusher-stemmer, it is inexpensive and does not adversely affect the quality of the finished wine.

Home winemakers who already own a crusher would do well to check its condition prior to arrival of grapes. If the unit is not of stainless steel construction, inspect all areas where fruit comes into contact with the equipment. Areas where rust is noted are excellent sites for metal contamination in the finished wine. If this is a problem, one would be well advised to apply a coat of food-grade epoxy enamel. These paints often involve special preparation prior to use, so attention should be given to instructions for mixing and for application temperatures.

A readily constructed stemmer for use in conjunction with older hand-operated crushers can be fashioned from a piece of chicken wire supported between four wooden slats, as schematically represented in Figure 1.

FIGURE 1a. Homemade stemmer consisting of a piece of chicken wire screen supported between four wooden slats.

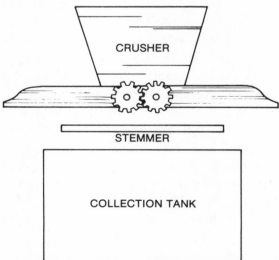

FIGURE 1b. Spatial arrangement of stemmer screen between crusher and collection tank.

The fruit collects between the crusher and receiving tank, and stem separation is achieved by gentle hand vibration. Again, this is a time-consuming alternative and care should be taken to prevent excessive stem buildup immediately below crusher rollers. However, with patience and frequent stem removal, adequate separation can be achieved. As with the crusher, care should be taken to enamel all areas before use.

Presses

Presses can also be expensive. The most commonly encountered press in the home operation is the basket model consisting of a slotted basket into which crushed grapes, or "pomace," are packed (Figure 2). Application of vertical pressure then forces the juice from the berries through the slotted basket and into a collection tray located beneath the press. Such models may be obtained at a cost ranging from $180 to $500, depending upon capacity and construction.

Alternately, one may elect to build his own press. The "rack and cloth" press is easily constructed as a shallow slotted box, the bottom and sides of which are lined with two layers of cheesecloth (Figure 3a). Pressure is then applied by means of a solid wooden insert placed on top. By addition of increasing weight, juice is squeezed from the berries into a collection tray below. An even simpler press can be made by collection of pomace into several thicknesses of cheesecloth. The corners are then tied to form a bag. In this case, juice is separated by rolling an object such as a rolling pin back and forth over the top of the bag. It is best to work on a slightly inclined surface so that the juice will collect into a receiving tray and not be reabsorbed into the pomace (Figure 3b). This simple press works especially well for pulpy fruits other than grapes.

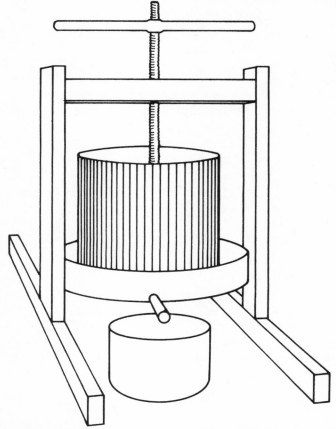

FIGURE 2. A typical basket press found in many home and some small commercial operations.

SOLID WOODEN INSERT

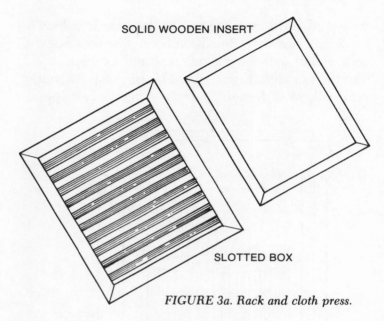

SLOTTED BOX

FIGURE 3a. Rack and cloth press.

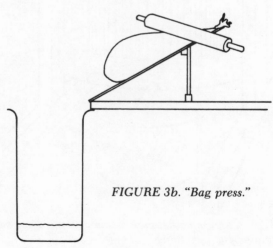

FIGURE 3b. "Bag press."

Fermentation and Storage Tanks

The fermentation facility may vary from wood or stainless steel barrels and tanks to five-gallon glass carboys for small lots of white wines. Some budget-minded winemakers have used plastic garbage cans as fermenters. However, because of the possibility of extraction of plasticizers, we recommend the use of only food approved polyethylene containers. These may sometimes be obtained from large restaurants or drive-ins, as well as restaurant supply houses.

Any metal storage or fermentation tanks which are of doubtful origin or composition should be inspected carefully before they are filled with juice or wine. Again, if rust spots are observed, it is essential to coat these areas with food-grade enamel. It is also worthwhile to check wooden tanks for internally exposed bolts or nails. In repair of older tanks we have found instances where these exposed metal surfaces have led to metal accumulations in the wine.

Filters

There are currently available several types of gravity-flow filters for small-lot operations. These are reasonably priced and may prove to be of value in your home plant. In lieu of these, however, careful racking, or the removal of sediment as it accumulates, will produce a very clear wine. Remember, clarification requires patience and if filtration is desired, one should not attempt it until the product is clear. The resultant

brilliant wine is, however, worth the extra time, effort
and cost.

Bottles and Corks

Both of these items are routinely available through
local wine supply stores. Since bottles may be readily
obtained from wine-consuming friends and restaurants, the purchase of new glass is a needless additional
cost. Glass has the advantage of being recyclable, and,
barring breakage, one should be able to develop a
stockpile of bottles in short order.

The money saved from not purchasing new glass is
wisely invested in the purchase of good quality corks.
Corks may be obtained in several grades as well as
lengths. Also, the winemaker may choose between
paraffin-coated and uncoated corks. For industrial
purposes, paraffin is applied to the cork to facilitate
high-speed closing machines. In addition, some feel
that a tighter seal is achieved by use of the paraffined
cork. As for cork length, it is generally agreed that 1.5-
inch cork is best for wines which will undergo additional bottle aging.

Prior to use, corks should be soaked for approximately twenty minutes in warm water. With the un-
paraffined cork, this accomplishes two goals. First,
soaking removes unwanted cork dust and debris and,
secondly, it softens the cork, thus facilitating easier
insertion into the bottle. After soaking, excess water
should be removed and the corks used before drying
can occur.

Winemakers frequently note that a wine may be only as good as the cork used at bottling. Since the purpose of the cork is to act as an effective barrier between the product and outside environment, we suggest that all corks be carefully screened for flaws prior to use. In that a major portion of the cost in production of small-lot wine is tied up in the purchase of cork, do not hesitate to spend an extra few cents for better quality closures. Use of inferior quality cork could and probably will result in disaster!

Corking Machines

The purpose of any corking machine, either manual, semiautomatic, or fully automatic, is to drive the cork flush into the neck of the bottle. The method of operation is relatively simple: the cork is compressed laterally by means of a set of jaws, and then driven into the bottle by a vertical plunger.

As far as we know, there is no alternative to the purchase of a corker. Since this piece of equipment is basic to the operation of any winery, we have included recommendations to aid in its purchase. A corker should have a spring-loaded, adjustable base plate to allow for closure of 1/5-gallon as well as 1/10-gallon bottles. Also, an adjustable plunger is useful to make minor adjustments in the depth of cork penetration. Finally, construction is important. Since you will be using this piece of equipment for years to come, it is best to invest a few extra dollars at this stage. Many seemingly inexpensive corkers on the market have a short life expectancy due to flaws in construction materials and workmanship.

Instead of cork-finish closures, many home winemakers utilize screw cap bottles and closures. Such containers are acceptable only for limited periods of storage. Prolonged aging in this type of container will result in noticeable oxidation of the wine.

Miscellaneous Supplies

Hydrometer: An absolute necessity for any operation is some means of determining the initial sugar or "Balling" of the fruit and monitoring its decrease with the ensuing fermentation. A more technically correct term for this measurement is "fermentable soluble solids." For all practical purposes, the winemaker considers 1° Balling approximately equal to 1% fermentable sugar.

A relatively inexpensive means of determining the fermentable soluble solids content is by use of the Balling or Brix hydrometer. Juice is simply collected in a cylinder in which the hydrometer is allowed to float freely. When a constant flotation level has been achieved, the fermentable soluble solids or "degrees Balling" is read directly on the spindle scale. Figure 4 depicts such a measurement. The sugar content of this fresh juice sample appears to be 24° B. In that the density of a fluid varies with temperature, it is important to carefully measure this parameter. The final soluble solids content should reflect a correction value of ± 0.033 for each one degree above or below the

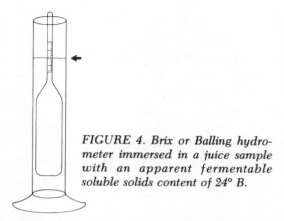

*FIGURE 4. Brix or Balling hydro-
meter immersed in a juice sample
with an apparent fermentable
soluble solids content of 24° B.*

hydrometer calibration temperature of 68° F. The cor-
responding value for a Centigrade thermometer is ±
0.06 for each one degree above or below 20° C. For
example, assume the juice has an apparent soluble solids content of 24° B. at a temperature of 80° F. Using
the correct value presented, the true reading should be
24.396. This value is correctly rounded off to 24.4° B.

Thus the effect of temperature is very important in
an accurate determination of initial fermentable sugar
content. As demonstrated in the above example, a
temperature difference of 12° F. from the calibration
temperature resulted in an increase of 0.4% fermentable sugar when compared with uncorrected apparent
values. This difference may become quite significant
as sample temperatures become more divergent from
68° F.

Residual Sugar Kits: Small amounts of fermentable
sugar may remain in the wine after the completion of
active fermentation. Even at these low levels, remain-

ing sugars may serve as a potential source of energy for spoilage yeast and bacteria. Thus, it is important for the professional and amateur winemaker alike to know the residual or reducing sugar content of his wine at bottling. While the small quantities of sugar are not usually measurable with hydrometers, they are readily determined by use of reducing sugar kits. Many home winemakers use the kits designed for diabetics. Each kit contains tablets that react with a measured amount of wine. The color of this reaction is then related to sugar content by means of a color index. Reducing-sugar tablets developed specially for wine are available through wine supply outlets at about the same cost as the diabetic kits. We recommend these because of their sensitivity and accuracy at sugar levels of less than one percent.

Sulfur Dioxide: Probably the most widely used chemical in the wine industry, sulfur dioxide, or SO_2, acts as an effective antioxidant in preventing browning in juice and wine as well as in inhibition of undesirable microbial activities. It also plays a role in color extraction in red grape varieties and juice clarification in white grape varieties.

Sulfur dioxide should always be added carefully, in that excessive amounts will inhibit normal alcoholic fermentation and produce off characters in the finished wine.

In small scale operations, the most efficient source of SO_2 is potassium metabisulfite. Since this chemical contains approximately 50% active SO_2 by weight, it is necessary to multiply your desired addition level by a factor of two in order to achieve the correct addition. Sulfur dioxide, as metabisulfite, should be added at the crushing stage and as necessary during subsequent processing operations. At crush, the recommended level for red wine fermentation is 100 parts per million (ppm) or 0.100 grams per kilogram of fresh fruit. By comparison, white wine fermentations usually require approximately 75 ppm or 0.075 grams per kilogram. Based on 100 pounds of red grapes, the sulfur dioxide addition at a level of 0.100 grams per kilogram may be calculated according to equation 1:

$$\frac{100 \text{ pounds}}{2.2} \times \frac{0.100 \text{ grams sulfur}}{\text{dioxide} \times 2} = \frac{9.09 \text{ grams}}{\text{metabisulfite}}$$

If you prefer to weigh the chemical in ounces, simply divide 9.09 grams by 28.3 grams per ounce. The resultant 0.32 ounces is approximately equivalent to one and one-half teaspoons of metabisulfite. The effectiveness of SO_2 in metabisulfite is limited under improper storage conditions. Therefore, one should plan to store this chemical in a dry location at room temperature.

Sulfur dioxide is also available in pellet form. The well-known Campden Tablet is widely used among home winemakers. As a rule of thumb, complete dissolution of one tablet into one gallon of wine yields an effective SO_2 concentration of approximately 65 ppm. Again, proper storage is essential if you plan to maintain a stock of tablets for future use.

Yeast and Yeast Starters: For production of high quality wines we do not recommend fermentation with "wild yeasts," or those occurring naturally on the grape. It has been our experience that these fermentations generally are slow in starting and produce inferior wines with many defects. It is suggested that the winemaker use one of several commercially available dry yeasts. These are commonly referred to as Wine-Active Dry Yeast or simply "WADY." The most frequently encountered strains of wine yeasts are Champagne and Montrachet. For most purposes, we have found the champage strain to be superior.

Prior to crush it is necessary to prepare a yeast "starter." This should be added to the crushed grapes or "must" at approximately 3% by volume. At this level, a clean, rapid fermentation with a minimum of off characters may normally be expected. To prepare the starter, collect the appropriate amount of juice and heat slowly to incipient boiling to destroy yeast and bacteria already present. Take care to prevent juice from burning. Cool rapidly to around 75° F. and add the dry yeast and nutrient. Yeast nutrient is generally a nitrogen-containing compound such as diammonium phosphate that stimulates yeast growth. When the starter is actively bubbling, usually within 30-45 minutes, proceed with the crush. At the completion of crushing operations, mix starter and must thoroughly.[1]

Nitrogen Gas: Since unfermented juice as well as wine is easily oxidized by contact with air, it is highly recommended that the winemaker invest in a cylinder of nitrogen gas. This gas is very effective in displacing oxygen from containers used in fermentation and wine transfer. Since oxidation is a common defect in homemade wines, we recommend liberal use of this gas in any operation where air may come into contact with the wine.

Nitrogen, in appropriate sized cylinders for home use, is available at most distributors of industrial and speciality gases. In addition to the cost of the gas, there is a demurage or rental charge placed on the cylinder when it leaves the premises. While this charge is usually assessed on a monthly basis, it is suggested that you return the empty cylinder as soon as possible to avoid incurring additional charges. A final note on safety is appropriate here. To avoid possible damage to cylinders, it is suggested that when not in use they be chained securely against an immovable object or positioned on their side and blocked firmly against the wall.

Wine Acids and Adjustments in Total Acidity: Proper acidity plays an important role in the character of the final wine. A wine of insufficient acidity will tend to taste flat and insipid whereas that same wine with a seemingly minor increase in acidity may become an exciting creation. Adjustment of wine and juice acidity plays an integral part in industrial operations but has, by and large, been overlooked in home winemaking. For this reason, we have included a brief consideration of the topic in this discussion.

First of all, it should be clearly understood that any adjustment in the acidity of either unfermented juice of finished wine should be made using only approved food-grade acids such as citric, malic or tartaric. These may be obtained through either wine or restaurant supply houses in most areas. Acid additions may take place either before fermentation or shortly before bottling. If you elect to adjust acidity prior to fermentation, we recommend the use of tartaric acid. Tartaric is the major acid occurring naturally in the grape. It has the added advantage of not being metabolized by most wine micro-organisms. The addition of tartaric acid to the finished wine is not suggested because of its decreased solubility in alcohol. Citric acid, on the other hand, is best and most commonly utilized in adjustment of acidity in finished wine prior to bottling. However, citric acid has the disadvantage of being utilized as a carbon source by wine bacteria and yeast.

In any adjustment of acidity, it is first necessary to know the quantity of acid present in the wine or juice. This is a routine analysis in any wine laboratory, but may create some difficulty in the home situation. A trip to your local wine supply store will likely solve this problem. There are currently on the market several kits designed for the home wine laboratory. These involve simple titration or neutralization of the acids in your sample with standardized base that is included in the kit. The so-called "endpoint of titration" is the point at which all the acidity has been neutralized by addition of base. The volume of base necessary to achieve this point is then related to the total acidity by a simple equation.

Wine acidity, expressed in grams of tartaric acid per 100 milliliters (ml) of sample, runs from very low (0.40) to medium (0.65) to high (0.90). Some wines produced in northern regions may exceed 1.0 gram per 100 ml but these excessively high acid wines are frequently unpalatable.

The mechanics of acid additions may best be demonstrated by means of a sample calculation. Assume you have a 10-gallon lot of clarified white grape juice with an initial acidity of 0.45 grams per 100 ml and you wish to increase the acidity to 0.65 grams per 100 ml. Using tartaric, the needed increase in acidity is 0.65 less 0.45, or 0.20 grams per 100 ml. This is equivalent to 2.0 grams per 1,000 ml or one liter. Using the simplified equation presented, one may readily calculate the necessary weight of acid to be added to any given gallonage of juice or wine:

Equation 2: $T = t \times 3.8 \times G$

In the above equation "T" is the unknown total weight, in grams, of tartaric acid that must be added, "t" is the desired acid increase, in grams per 1,000 ml, and "G" is the gallonage of juice or wine. Using the specific example of a 2.0 gram per 1,000 ml addition to 10 gallons of juice, the correct weight of tartaric acid needed is 76 grams. Converting to the English system of measure, simply divide 76 grams by 453.6 grams per pound, or 28.3 grams per ounce. The result is 0.17 pounds or 2.7 ounces, respectively. If you choose to use either citric or malic acid instead of tartaric, it is necessary to multiply your final weight by a factor of 0.853 for citric and 0.893 for malic.

It should be pointed out that in determining the volume of juice to acidify, one should use only clarified product. Thus, it is best to hold the lot under refrigeration overnight to allow the solids to settle⁀ from solution. The following morning, then, the clarified juice is siphoned or "racked" from the sediment and the final volume determined. Using glass carboys, volume determination may be accomplished by use of either a measuring device or by weight, knowing that one gallon of juice is approximately equal to eight pounds. A convenient measuring rod, made of wooden dowel and marked off in liters or gallons, can easily be prepared by pouring measured quantities of water into a carboy and marking the volume after each addition. Alternately, a measuring tape prepared for this purpose is presented in Figure 5.

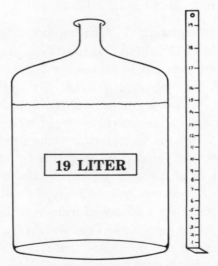

FIGURE 5. A simple measuring device for volume determination. Note that this tape is marked off in liters to simplify necessary calculations.

As a concluding word on acids, we should mention that the cost difference between the three recommended products is significant. Tartaric acid is currently listed at $1.07 per pound whereas citric and malic acids are $0.72 and $0.71 per pound respectively. In some cases, price alone may dictate which acid a winemaker may select. However, we feel that tartaric is far superior to either citric or malic acid.

Cooperage: Another important consideration under the topic of winemaking supplies is cooperage. The use of wooden containers for fermentation and storage of wine is not a recent development. Wine historians report the use of barrel-like storage vessels to date to at least the first century A.D., and possibly earlier. Despite the availability of better types of storage, modern-day winemakers still use wood, principally oak, redwood, and, on rare occasion, chestnut, for fermentation, aging, and storage of wine. Of the available types of wood, oak is, by far, the choice of modern day winemakers.

Unfortunately for the novice and, on occasion, the professional cellar master, preparation and maintenance of barrels is oftentimes problematic and fraught with pitfalls that can render good cooperage unusable. Since many of the problems in homemade wines are directly attributable to the aging step, we feel the need to expand and more fully develop this area.

Since the terminology of the cooper is somewhat unique and, generally speaking, alien to the novice, we have included the following figure which identifies the principal components of a typical barrel. For con-

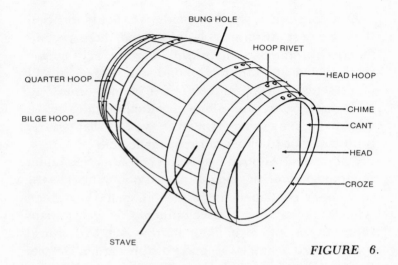

FIGURE 6.

venience, the glossary at the end of this book more
formally defines each component.

Before discussing the special attributes of oak that
make it a sought-after storage container, it would be
useful to discuss what oak aging accomplishes. Oak
aging is, in reality, a slow and controlled oxidation
process, bringing about the maturation of young wines
by reaction and marrying of wine components with
those in the oak. Visually and organoleptically, the
most notable changes that occur in wine during aging
are in color, astringency, and flavor. In the case of
young red wines, this may be visualized as a slow
change in the deep purple color of the young wine to
those tints characteristic of age. Concomittantly, astringent phenolics condense and precipitate from solution

yielding a wine with a perceivably soft character. Although we have described barrel aging as a slow and controlled oxidation, air probably comes into contact with aging wine as a result of routine racking or topping operations rather than through pores in the wood.

The desirability of oak as compared to other available woods such as redwood or pine, stems in part from its density. With age, the woody center of the oak tree loses its conductive role and becomes hardened, yielding what is termed "heartwood." Heartwood consists principally of hemicellulose and cellulosic elements which contribute to the structural attributes of oak. Further, cells in the heartwood that formerly were conductive in nature become plugged with tylosic intrusions. These serve as blocks and effectively prevent or slow free flow of liquid. It is this nonporous character that makes heartwood ideal for barrel staves. Among oaks, the extent of stave porosity seems to vary with the species and origin of the particular oak. In general, European species of oak tend to have fewer intrusions and are therefore more porous than their American counterparts.

Owing to the vascular character of oak, there is a more-or-less one-way transport of wine components from the inside out. This allows small molecules like water and alcohol to differentially escape from the wine while minimizing the entrance of oxygen. Movement of alcohol and water out of the barrel is dependent upon the ambient relative humidity in the cellar. If the relative humidity is more than 65 to 70%, alcohol

tends to escape from the wine faster than water, whereas at less than 60%, water escapes faster. In the range 60-
65%, both water and alcohol escape at more or less the
same rate. Loss of water and alcohol from the wine is
visually apparent as the presence of headspace or "ullage" that may develop in barrel aging wine. In a tightly
bunged barrel, translocation of water and alcohol results in a slight negative pressure (vacuum) forming in
this headspace.

Several types of oak are currently available to the
winemaker. These include American, French, German,
and, on occasion, Yugoslavian. Upon casual consideration one might think that all oaks are more or less
similar. However, if you were to poll winemakers you
would find a good deal of disagreement as to which is
best for any one purpose. Further, modern-day winemakers recognize the important contributions of the
cooper and, therefore, may go as far as to specify the
individual cooper that they want to make their barrels.

Initially, climatic and soil conditions affect the growing patterns of oak forests. Generally, cool growing
conditions favor increased density of the sought-after
heartwood layer. Further, the level of extractives contributing to the oak character seems to concentrate in
oaks from cooler areas as compared to those grown in
warmer climates.

The species of oak appears to be an important consideration in selection of cooperage. Largely because of
availability, three species of oak are most frequently
used for cooperage. These include *Quercus alba*, the

American oak, and the European oaks, Q. *robur* and Q. *sessilis.*

Organoleptically, there appear to be significant differences at least between American and European oaks. Winemakers often describe the character of American oak as being decidedly "assertive" as compared with its more subtle and refined European counterparts. Therefore, wines aged in fresh American oak typically have a noticeable and distinct oak character as well as a measure of coarseness. However, this may be mitigated somewhat by coopering technique.

Of late, many winemakers report that while the species of oak may be important in the nature and level of organoleptically important extractives, the methodology of coopering is of at least equal, if not greater importance. The following short discussion of barrel making may cast some light on the difference between coopering styles.

Aside from the species of oak used, the initial drying phase of fresh-cut wood is thought to be an important difference between coopers. American coopers typically use kiln-dried oak while their European counterparts traditionally use wood that has been air-dried for two to four years. The practice of lengthy air drying is believed to moderate the excessive coarse extractives that are thought to be a problem in American oak.

American coopering technique uses staves that have been sawn as compared with European style of splitting each stave. While this probably plays a minor role in the aging process, the method of forming the staves is a major and significant difference between the styles.

American coopers form or bend staves by exposure to steam and fire or, in some cases, steam alone. By comparison, the European cooper uses fire to form staves. Forming staves over an open flame is believed to moderate excessive astringency as well as yielding the so-called "toasty character" that is sought-after by some winemakers for development of wine bouquet in certain varieties such as Chardonnay and Sauvignon Blanc. Winemakers' opinions as to the extent of toasting vary depending upon wine type, vintage, and style. In certain instances, the winemaker may specify aging in lightly toasted barrels, whereas in other cases a heavier toast may be thought to be appropriate.

The intentional charring of the barrel's inner surfaces has an important drawback in that it produces irregular surfaces and crevices that serve as collection sites for wine yeast and bacteria. Thus, this technique creates secondary problems in proper cleaning and sanitizing the barrel after use. This is not as much a problem in staves formed by steam.

When considering the acquisition of cooperage for the home cellar, one is initially faced with the problem of cost versus return. New cooperage is, obviously, more expensive than used and may require more extensive treatment prior to holding wine. As of this writing, new sixty-gallon French Nevers and Limuosine oak barrels cost about two and one-half times more than new American oak cooperage of the same volume. Frequently wineries will sell their cooperage, including European barrels, after one or two vintages. Such cooperage may, in many instances, be obtained at less than half the cost of new cooperage. However, one should consider the risk, in these cases, of buying barrels already contaminated with spoilage bacteria and/or yeast. We recommend bringing a flashlight and a reasonably functional olfactory system along on purchasing trips. Cooperage with excessive tartrate precipitation and odd odors should be rejected outright and others in the lot evaluated very carefully. Properly stored used cooperage will probably have a rather strong odor of sulfur dioxide that will very quickly irritate the eyes and nasal passages. Therefore, caution should be exercised when one evaluates freshly opened barrels. To conclude our comments on used cooperage, it should be pointed out that while the price may be attractive, there is generally no guarantee as to whether the wood is sound and, therefore, the winemaker is advised, *Caveat Emptor*!

Whether you decide to use new or used, domestic or foreign cooperage, there are several preliminary steps that should be taken to prepare the barrel to receive wine. In the case of used barrels, several thorough washings in tap water are generally all that is required. New wood, however, because of its high content of unstable tannins, needs to be extensively treated prior to filling with wine. It is recommended that the barrel be repeatedly filled with water and drained for several days or until all leaks have sealed and the "green wood" character is gone. Toward the end of the swelling period, the use of hot water may help to reduce the undesirable coarse characters of the new wood. Do not firmly set the hoops until the swelling process is complete. At this time, a few gentle taps with a hoop driver should take care of any minor leaks that may be seen. If continued leakage is noted, it must be stopped prior to adding the wine. Since this subject is covered later in this chapter, we will only point out here that if the barrel will not hold water without leaking, the likelihood of it successfully holding wine is not great.

Upon removal of wine late in the year, cooperage should be carefully rinsed and excess water allowed to drain. Depending upon the length of time the barrel will be stored before refilling with wine or must, two storage techniques are available. For short-term storage, we suggest burning a single sulfur stick per fifty gallons. Dripless sulfur sticks are readily available at nominal cost. Sulfur sticks should be suspended from the lower side of the bung, ignited, and carefully inserted into the barrel. When expired, the stick should be quickly removed and a fresh bung inserted firmly. Occasionally, portions of the stick may fall into the barrel. These should be removed immediately. A handy accessory for the barrel sulfuring operation is a sulfur cup, which not only prevents the burnt stick from fragmenting into the barrel but also retains any melted sulfur that may drip from the stick. Sulfur cups are available commercially but can easily be constructed at home with a piece of stainless steel wire and a screw cap from a one-gallon jug. Figure 6A schematically represents such a homemade sulfur cup, which, based on our experience, is adequate.

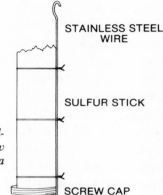

STAINLESS STEEL
WIRE

SULFUR STICK

FIGURE 6A. Homemade barrel-sulfuring cup composed of a screw cap from a one-gallon jug and a piece of stainless steel wire.

SCREW CAP

After sulfuring is completed, barrel wax should be applied to seal any apparent discontinuities between bung and barrel. When sulfuring is used to stabilize cooperage, it should be inspected regularly to ensure fully active sulfur dioxide is still present.

The above technique suffers from the problem that with time the wood dehydrates, thereby creating potential for leaks. For longer-term storage barrels should be filled with a solution of 600 mg/liter sulfur dioxide (as potassium metabisulfite) *and* 1.25% citric acid. The inclusion of the citric acid is *absolutely essential* in that it shifts the acidity of the water-sulfur dioxide solution so that the antimicrobial form (sulfur dioxide) is present and fully active. Failure to include the citric acid will result guaranteed spoilage due to an assortment of microbes. Once this has happened, these barrels cannot be reused without extensive and expensive treatment at the cooperage house.

Barrel closure usually involves the use of some sort of stopper, called a "bung." Traditionally, wooden bungs, either of oak or redwood, are used for this purpose. Owing to the relative softness of the wood, coopers often recommend the use of redwood rather than oak bungs to effect a tight seal without damage to the barrel. In the case of woods other than oak, however, wickering effects may be seen. That is, wine is drawn from inside the barrel, through the pores, forming beads on the top surface of the bung. This serves as a site for the growth of acetic acid bacteria and spoilage yeast as well as attracting fruit flies. The problem may be corrected by the use of special sealants. Food grade epoxy paints are available to seal areas of bung that come into contact with the wine.

Another problem inherent to the use of wooden bungs is forming a tight seal between stopper and bunghole. Unless a perfect seal is effected, headspace ("ullage") will quickly develop in the barrel and its contents will oxidize. As mentioned in the preceding paragraph, cellar workers frequently utilize barrel wax to overcome this problem. However, in addition to being unsightly, wax also serves as an excellent site to trap spoilage organisms.

Today, many winemakers are successfully using silicon bungs instead of wood. In addition to overcoming the problems associated with wooden bungs, they seem to effect tighter seals and are easily cleaned and sanitized when necessary.

Problems Associated with Oak Cooperage: Growth

of spoilage organisms in barrel aging wines is not a problem restricted to the home winemaker. Commercial wineries with extensive oak storage on occasion experience the same problems. Two groups of microorganisms are most troublesome in this regard. The oxidative or "film" yeast grow on the surface of aging wines that are exposed to air. These are visually the easiest spoilage yeasts to detect. Growing as a surface film in barrel-aging wine that has not been properly "topped off," these yeast with time produce a very apparent oxidative or sherry-like character in the wine.

Control of oxidative surface yeast is most easily effected by routine topping to eliminate ullage and, hence, the source of oxygen needed for growth. Another spoilage yeast that is much more difficult to control and presently of greater concern to the winemaker is *Brettanomyces*. Wines tainted by the growth of this organism are typically described as having a "wet dog" or "open sewer" character. "Bret," as it is affectionately known, grows rather slowly and without the obvious film character of surface yeasts. Because of this growth pattern, the yeast may easily go undetected until well after the wine has spoiled. Since its growth is not as apparent as that of film-formers, contaminated wine may easily be spread throughout the winery in normal cellar operations, and from winery to winery upon sale of bulk wine. The problem is compounded in that Bret is not particularly sensitive to sulfur dioxide at routine use levels. Control of this organism lies in exclusion from the cellar rather than corrective action an already established population. Sanitation and scrupulous examination of wines and cooperage entering the cellar are essential in preventing its appearance and growth.

Among the bacteria that cause problems in barrel aging of wines are the acetics. These aerobic or oxygen-requiring bacteria grow as a film at the surface of wine only when there is a source of oxygen. Control of acetics is the same as with film yeast. That is, a proper topping routine must be followed so that ullage does not form. Additionally, maintenance of proper levels of sulfur dioxide will serve as a deterrent to the growth of acetics as well as lactic bacteria present in aging wines. Usually levels approaching 100 ppm (total sulfur dioxide) are adequate for control.

Assuming the barrel does not become contaminated with spoilage yeasts or acetic acid bacteria, wood cooperage still has a limited life. With normal aging of red wines, pigments and tartrates precipitate from the wines and block the extractive and aging surface of the barrel. With each vintage, more surface area is lost and, eventually, the barrel becomes little more than a storage container. If a cooper is available, the barrel can be taken apart and shaved to expose fresh aging surface and thus extend its useful life.

Professional and amateur cellarmasters, alike, often experience the problem of leaky cooperage. The problem may be as simple as leaks at the end of staves resulting from the wickering effect to cracked staves that result from dropping the barrel. Stave-end leaks are frequently a problem, especially in the case of new European oak. As pointed out earlier, these oaks tend to be more porous than American species and therefore often exhibit a wickering effect with the result that wine may seep through the ends of staves. Some European coopers deal with this problem by painting the stave ends. Cellar personnel often deal with minor seeping by preparing a bentonite-water solution and filling the troublesome barrel with it. After a few hours, the problem is usually corrected.

In the case of larger leaks, several epoxy preparations, collectively called "wet surface liners," are available to deal temporarily with the problem until a cooper can replace the damaged stave. These have the advantage that they can be applied to damp surfaces. However, these should be regarded as only temporary measures.

Woodboring beetles (*Scobicia declivis*) infest oaks and other hardwoods throughout the hills and mountains of the western United States. Unfortunately for winemakers, woodboring beetles may also attack oak cooperage. Adults of this species are dark brown, resembling a hump-backed grain of rice. After mating, the female bores a tunnel into the tree (or barrel) where she lays her egg. In two to three weeks, the larva hatches and continues to bore into the wood. The result is a tunnel with a diameter approximating that of a pencil lead. The larva then pupates and eventually emerges from its home as the adult.

Unless controlled, emergent adults may reinfest the

same barrel. Control measures include general cleanup of the storage and surrounding areas to remove brush and wood to which the adults may be attracted and hide. Surface preparations are available that when applied act as both a mildewicide and insecticide. In the case of new or used cooperage that has already been damaged, toothpicks inserted into the tunnel(s) will generally correct the problem with minimal cost. Alternatively, one may purchase conical wooden dowels ("spikes") that accomplish the same goal.

After having read the preceding several pages, the home winemaker is probably considering options other than aging in oak barrels. This may not be such a bad idea. First of all, consider that many winemakers, today, are deemphasizing the oak character. Varieties that traditionally received moderate to heavy oak aging are finished with much reduced levels. The reasons for this are no doubt varied. Knowledgeable consumers today appreciate a more refined balance of fruit and oak. Additionally, cost of purchase and maintenance of oak barrels has dramatically increased. Further, the winemaker is faced with the much greater potential for spoilage.

Several alternatives to barrel aging are available to the winemaker. These include the use of oak chips and specially produced oak extracts. Contrary to popular belief, the proper use of oak chips may produce a wine that is difficult to distinguish from one aged in the barrel. Further, chips are convenient in that they may be discarded when the desired effects have been achieved, thus avoiding bothersome barrel maintenance. Take note, however, that for best results, chips must be processed prior to contact with wine. This is done in a manner similar to that used in preparing green cooperage. Collect several handfuls of chips into a one-gallon, wide-mouth glass container, fill with hot water, and allow to soak for several days. You will probably note that the water quickly becomes discolored. During the soaking period, the water should be regularly drained and replaced with fresh. After two or three days, or when the raw wood character has dissipated, the chips should be air dried prior to use. Some vintners include as one of the last rinses a citric acid wash using 1.25% citric acid. In this case, however, at least two rinses in hot water should follow to neutralize the acid. After thoroughly drying the chips, transfer to several gallon jugs or a carboy and add the wine. Where chips are used commercially, addition levels range from 2-7 pounds per thousand gallons or, converting to a fifty-gallon lot, 2-6 ounces.

We do not recommend adding chips to the entire volume of wine. Rather, we suggest preparation of an oak extract concentrate for later blending with the total volume. For a fifty-gallon lot, two gallons of oak extract are recommended. Store wine and chips at room temperature for several weeks, or until a heavy oak character is developed. Remember, you are preparing an oak extract for blending, and therefore, the oak character, which will be subsequently diluted, must be much greater than you would normally want. After the desired effect has been achieved, decant the wine from chips and blend into your untreated wine at the desired level.

Several brands of prepared oak extracts are commercially available. While many of the early attempts to produce extracts resulted in less than desirable effects, recent products that we have reviewed appear to be adequate. As testimony to the quality of these products, many wineries are currently blending finished wines with oak extract rather than investing in costly cooperage. Using these extracts, one simply prepares a series of trials with different levels of extract, evaluates each relative to the untreated lot, and extrapolates the desired level to the final volume of wine.

Transfer Hoses: An absolute necessity for any operation is some means of conveying wine from one container to another. In small lot operations, this may be best achieved by means of several feet of flexible plastic tubing which can be purchased from most pet stores. For routine work, select tubing with an inside diameter of one-quarter to one-half inch, depending upon the quantity of wine you plan to make.

Since the siphon is flexible, it is best to attach it, with several rubber bands, to a piece of wood doweling for support. As demonstrated in Figure 7, this allows you to direct the intake suction as necessary to avoid excessive sediment pickup which is encountered in early rackings. Since you may want to use the siphon without the dowel at a later date, it is suggested that the intake end be notched to prevent adherence

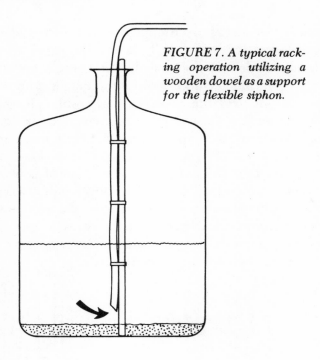

FIGURE 7. A typical rack-
ing operation utilizing a
wooden dowel as a support
for the flexible siphon.

to sides of containers. Wine residues serve as excellent
sites for microbial growth and contamination. Therefore racking hoses should be thoroughly rinsed and
allowed to drain after use.

Fermentation Locks: During active fermentation,
carbon dioxide evolution is maximum and fermentation locks usually are not needed. During this stage of
processing, openings in fermenters can be simply covered with a clean piece of cloth to prevent fruit flies
and debris from falling into the wine. However, as
carbon dioxide evolution ceases at the completion of

alcoholic fermentation, the air pressure surrounding the fermentation vessel will exceed the pressure of carbon dioxide being given off. As a result, air will enter the fermenter and come into contact with the wine, causing oxidation to occur. This problem is most easily overcome by use of a fermentation or "gas lock." As shown in Figure 8a, fermentation locks are available in a variety of shapes and sizes. They all accomplish the same goal, the prevention of contact between wine and oxygen by interposition of a water barrier. Any pressure buildup inside the container which exceeds atmospheric pressure will escape. However, since air pressure outside the fermenter is not as great, the reverse cannot occur.

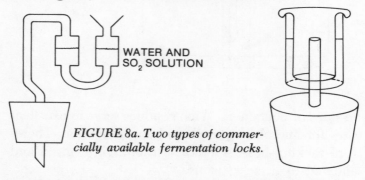

WATER AND
SO_2 SOLUTION

FIGURE 8a. Two types of commercially available fermentation locks.

Although fermentation locks are relatively inexpensive, there are alternatives. The most simple of these is the insertion of a piece of flexible plastic tubing through the cork closure into the headspace above the fermentation. The outlet is then immersed into a gallon jug filled to three-quarters capacity with a solution of potassium metabisulfite and water (Figure 8b). If you are fermenting in glass carboys, another popular alternative is the use of a balloon stretched over the neck opening (Figure 8c). As carbon dioxide pressure builds, the balloon expands to a point where vents are created between the rubber and glass, resulting in collapse.

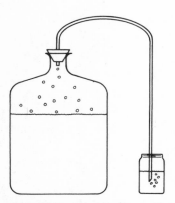

FIGURE 8b. Homemade alternative utilizing a quart jar and a piece of small diameter hose.

FIGURE 8c. At completion of alcoholic fermentation, a balloon may be stretched over the mouth of container to allow escape of remaining gas.

Now that we have presented an introduction to the necessary equipment and supplies needed in production of wine, we can proceed with a discussion of several types of wine which can easily be produced in your own cellar.

2

FRUIT WINE PRODUCTION

FROM THE EARLY PART OF JUNE through most of the summer, berries, plums, peaches, apricots and other fresh fruit products are readily available to the home winemaker. Wines made from these products present an interesting complement to the grape wines you will be making in the later part of the summer and autumn. Fruit wines do, however, require special attention and processing techniques which will be considered in the following paragraphs.

Crushing: Berries, apples and the like are easily crushed with the same crusher that you will be using in grape wine production. Maceration of pitted fruits, however, may create difficulty if your crusher does not have provision for opening the gap between the rollers. If this can be accomplished without a major overhaul of your equipment, the rollers should be adjusted so that only the largest pits are ruptured, leaving the smaller ones to pass through undamaged. Approximately one percent of the pits should be cracked. Since much of the character of certain fruit wines, especially apricot, is contained within the pit, failure to take advantage of this may result in a product that is deficient in character. If crackage exceeds 1.5-2%, however, a decidedly bitter character may be imparted into the wine. In lieu of crusher modification, fruit may simply be cut into quarters and halves with a paring knife. It has been our experience that even pieces this large will distintegrate under the effect of full fermentation.

Certain fruits, especially apples, peaches, and apricots, are subject to rapid enzymatic browning. This is most readily demonstrated by halving an apple and leaving it exposed to the air. The same reaction accompanies the crushing of any fruit, but is more visible in the varieties identified. To lessen the effects of oxidation, we suggest an addition of sulfur dioxide at a level of 0.100 grams per kilogram of fruit at crush. Also, a liberal injection of nitrogen gas directly into the crushed fruit is recommended at this stage.

The Addition of Water: Fruits such as plums and peaches may be excessively high in acid. In the case of fruit other than grapes, the government allows commercial wineries to reduce the total acidity to 0.50 grams per 100 ml with water in order to achieve a more palatable product. However, this addition may not exceed 35% of the total volume of crushed fruit. In the case of loganberries, boysenberries, gooseberries and currants, this level may be as high as 60% of the crush volume. Without addition of water it is, in fact, difficult to achieve a measurable juice yield. The quantity of water to be added is easily calculated with the use of a simple scale. Assuming an initial 10 pounds of crushed loganberries, the addition of 53% water allows us to add up to 5.3 pounds of water. Pounds of water is converted to gallons; one gallon of water weighs 8 pounds. Thus, to 10 pounds of fruit we can add 0.7 gallons of water.

The Addition of Sugar: Peaches, plums, and berries

normally have 12-14% fermentable sugar at harvest. Assuming a conversion of sugar to alcohol as 0.5%, this will yield from 6-7% alcohol when fermented to dryness. Therefore, it is necessary to add a measured amount of sugar to increase the final alcohol yield. The sample calculation presented below is based on 10 pounds of freshly crushed fruit with an initial fermentable sugar content, measured in degrees Balling, of 12°. Allowing ourselves a maximum amelioration of 53% water, the final weight of fruit and water becomes 15.3 pounds. Further, we wish the final alcohol to be 10% (v/v). Since 1° B. is converted to approximately 0.5% alcohol upon complete fermentation, the final sugar content for the unfermented material must be 20° B. The extra quantity of sugar that must be added to the fermentation may be easily calculated using Equations 3A and 3B presented below:

(A) initial sugar = $\dfrac{\text{pounds of fruit}}{2.2}$ x 12° B. x 10

(B) desired sugar = $\dfrac{\text{pounds of fruit} + \text{water}}{2.2}$ x 20° B. x 10

Subtraction of equation B from equation A: 1390 grams - 545.5 grams = 844.5 grams, and converting to pounds of sugar: $\dfrac{844.5 \text{ grams}}{453.6 \text{ grams per pound}}$ or, 1.9 pounds of sugar.

The addition of sugar to a fruit wine fermentation is usually not done in lump form. Rather, equal portions are added at regular intervals until the calculated amount has been exhausted. The addition of sugar in this manner is termed "syruping." A word of caution is needed here. Since sugar tends to lump together, we recommend folding the sugar into the fermentation as you would with the components of a cake batter.

Fermentation and Pressing: Recommended temperatures for the fermentation of fruit wines are approximately those of white wines, from 55° - 65° F. When the desired color and flavor are achieved, the "cap"— solids that have risen to the top of the fermentation as a result of carbon dioxide gas evolution—is removed and pressed as discussed in introductory considerations. The liquid portion, or "free run," is transferred to five-gallon carboys and the final portion of sugar added. Be careful not to fill containers more than three-quarters because continued fermentation will, in short order, cause overflow. At this point, determine the sugar content by hydrometer and monitor daily until fermentation has completed. The "press wine," or that portion derived from the cap after pressing, is usually maintained separately and blended back into the final wine at a later date. In the later stages of fermentation, gaseous evolution will decrease. It is essential at this time to prevent air from entering the fermentation vessel and coming into contact with the wine. Protection is most easily achieved by use of fermentation locks, or their alternatives, as discussed in the preceding chapter. As hydrometer readings approach zero, monitor the utilization of remaining fermentable sugars by use of reducing sugar tablets. Remember, there is very little gaseous evolution occurring at this stage. Therefore, a thorough sparging of the headspace above the wine with nitrogen is a recommended practice after drawing samples.

As active fermentation slows and finally stops, yeast settles out of solution as a thick whitish sediment called "lees." Since these will contribute off characters to the wine, it is absolutely essential that large quantities of lees not be allowed to accumulate. Their removal is easily effected by siphoning the clarifying wine away from the sediment, a process called "racking." It is generally best, although not essential, to hold the wine at low temperatures during the clarification stage. After the first racking, it is routine practice to make a sulfur dioxide addition at a level of 0.030 grams per liter according to Equation 1. You should not consider filtration until the product is clear. This stage should be reached within six weeks after racking. Remember, the goal of filtration is to produce a brilliant wine and proceeding before adequate clarification has occurred will only result in a clogged filter. In many cases, home winemakers prefer to clarify through continued racking rather than to invest money in filtration equipment.

Bottling: Fruit wines generally do not benefit from aging as do their grape counterparts. Therefore, when your wine has reached the desired degree of clarity, it is time to bottle. Most people prefer to sweeten their product with sugar prior to bottling. Unless you plan either to hold the wine under continuous refrigeration or to add a preservative, this is not recommended, since any yeasts remaining in the wine will, in short order, ferment the added sugar and spoil the product. Assuming you are going to bottle a sweetened wine, the normally used preservative is sorbic acid, sold as potassium sorbate. The recommended level for stability is 0.350 grams per liter. A simplified calculation for a typical sorbic acid addition at this level is presented in Equation 4.

$$\text{Grams of Sorbic Acid Needed} = 0.350 \times \frac{150}{112} \times 3.8 \times \underline{\quad\quad} \text{ gallons of wine}$$

At this step you should also plan to add sulfur dioxide, as metabisulfite, at a level of 0.030 grams per liter according to Equation 1.

All wines, immediately after bottling, suffer from what is commonly called "bottle sickness." This simply refers to an out-of-balance condition that results from preparing the wine for bottling. Therefore, one should not plan to consume the product for at least four weeks after bottling.

Agricultural Wines

By government definition, an agricultural wine is one made from "products other than the juice of fruit." This wine category includes products made from dried fruits such as raisins, figs, and the like as well as honey or mead wines. The few examples of agricultural wines that we have seen in home winemaking competition have left a great deal to be desired. This is largely because special processing techniques are required to handle initially high sugar levels and, in the case of dried fruit products, initial browning.

Raisin Wines

Since the sugar content of raisins is high, about 75 to 80° B., an initial dilution with water is required to insure successful fermentation. Commercially, the winemaker is allowed to reduce the initial sugar content of the raisin with water to that of the fresh fruit. However, this cannot be less than 22° B. As a "rule of thumb," this dilution amounts to three parts water per one part raisins. Such dilutions are best done on a weight basis; remember, one gallon of water weighs eight pounds. Sulfur dioxide additions should be made at a level of 0.100 grams per kilogram at this stage.

Fermentation of reconstituted raisin "must" should be carried out under cool conditions, usually 55-60° F., using a 3% (v/v) active starter of wine yeasts. As is the case with any wine, care must be taken to prevent lees accumulation and unnecessary oxidation in post-fermentation processing. Raisin wines are best finished slightly sweet to sweet with the addition of from 1-6% sucrose (cane sugar). As with fruit wines, the preservative potassium sorbate must be added to the sweetened wine to prevent refermentation. Calculations and recommended levels of addition have already been discussed.

A final word of caution regarding the use of dried fruits is appropriate. The winemaker should avoid the use of "bleached" fruit such as raisins sold under the designation "golden." The bleaching process is accomplished by the addition of large quantities of sulfur (1000-1500 mg/l) which even upon preliminary dilution will inhibit fermentation.

Honey Wines (Mead)

Wine historians suggest that the first fermented beverage was probably honey. While we prefer to avoid conjecture on this point, we have found mead to be a popular product with the home winemaking set. Mead may be produced in two styles, (1) the traditional heavy-sweet dessert type, and (2) light-bodied and slightly sweet table wine. In either case, the honey must be diluted to approximately 22° B. prior to fermentation. Furthermore, since the product is deficient in nutrient and acidity, supplementation of these components is required. Acid addition is best carried out with citric acid at recommended levels of 18.9 grams per gallon of diluted product. To this, 5.6 grams of yeast nutrient, as diammonium phosphate, and sulfur dioxide, as potassium metabisultite, at 0.100 grams per liter are added. Using remaining diluted honey, an active yeast starter is prepared and added at 3% (v/v) when actively foaming. Honey wine should be fermented at 65-75° F. to reduce the possibility of stalling during fermentation. (This is referred to as a "stuck" fermentation.)

Post fermentation processing is as we have already discussed in preceding sections. Mead is probably at its best when finished with 4-7% cane sugar or undiluted honey. It is recommended that this addition be made to the final product immediately prior to bottling. Included in finishing operations is the addition of potassium sorbate at 0.350 grams per liter and sulfur dioxide at 0.030 grams per liter. Instructions for these additions have already been presented in Chapters 1 and 2. Occasionally, mead is produced as a heavy-bodied dessert style wine. In this case, the product may be sweetened and fortified with a high quality vodka to desired alcohol levels, usually around 18% (v/v). Simplified fortification calculations are described in Chapter 4. It should be noted that commercially the practice of fortifying non-fruit fermented beverages is not allowed. However, this restriction is not an important consideration to the amateur enologist.

3

TABLE WINE PRODUCTION

THE PRODUCTION OF GRAPE WINES differs somewhat from fruit wines. Most importantly, California regulations prohibit the addition of either sugar or water to the juice in order to acheive a better balance in the final product. Therefore, care must be taken in determination of fruit maturity at time of harvest. Usually it is recommended that white varieties not be harvested until the sugar level reaches 23-24° Balling. Red varieties, on the other hand, are generally not harvested until their sugar content reaches 24-25° Balling. These levels are required for adequate berry maturity and development of varietal character. Traditionally, dessert wine varieties have been harvested at higher sugar levels. Grapes destined for port and muscatel fermentations should be harvested at 25-27° Balling, or higher, contingent upon berry quality.

Examination of the wine merchant's shelf will show increasing numbers of wines with the label designation "Late Harvest." This indicates that the grapes going into the wine were allowed to develop to maximum maturity, in some cases up to 35-38° Balling, before crush. Due to the abnormally high initial sugar content, the alcoholic fermentation is, from the outset, stressed and yeast metabolism ceases before all the sugar is converted to alcohol. The result is a naturally sweet wine with 13-14% alcohol that is stable with respect to further yeast fermentation.

It has recently been recognized that acidity, in addition to sugar, plays an important role in the balance of the final wine. Thus, the informed vintner must consider the balance of sugar and acid, or the so-called "sugar-acid ratio" at harvest. However, since the determination of acidity may involve supplies not readily available to the average home operator, the sugar content may serve as your best index of maturity. In the selection of berries for a sugar determination, try to randomize the collection, including samples from several vines as well as different locations on the vine and grape cluster. As a general rule, 100 berries are collected per sample. These should be crushed thoroughly to yield a homogenous sample. As a useful hint, we have found electric blenders to be ideal for this purpose. After blending, the puree is collected between several thicknesses of cheesecloth and the juice strained into a collection vessel. The sugar content may then be determined by use of a Balling or Brix hydrometer.

White Grape Wines

Crushing: Prior to crush one should select out damaged or moldy grapes as well as extraneous materials such as leaves, canes, etc. At crush, it is normal practice to add sulfur dioxide, as potassium metabisulfite, to prevent browning and other spoilage related problems as discussed under that topic. Assuming good quality grapes, you should plan to make your SO_2 addition at a level of 0.075 grams per kilogram of fresh fruit according to Equation 1. By comparison to red wines, juice destined for white wine production is, in most cases, pressed from the skins with minimal or no contact time. Certain varieties, namely Chardonnay, Gewurtztraminer, and Muscat require a short period of fermentation "on the skins" in order to bring out their varietal character and intensity. Since excessive tannin levels are objectionable in white wines, this contact period usually lasts only 6-12 hours, at which time pressing occurs.

Pressing: In a large-scale operation, the press cake, or "sweet pomace," is utilized further as distillation material or "DM" in production of fortifying alcohol or beverage brandy. Since the amateur winemaker is generally not production oriented, we recommend a gentle press, sacrificing yield for the quality of juice.

Juice Clarification: It is generally agreed that white wines fermented from clarified juice are superior to those fermented immediately after pressing with a high solids content. Therefore, except in those cases cited where short-termed fermentation occurs in the presence of skins, it is recommended that the juice be allowed to clarify overnight. This should be accomplished at refrigeration temperatures to prevent incipient fermentation from wild yeasts. In the morning, then, the clarified juice is siphoned free from the sediment.

Fermentation: As is normally the case, a yeast starter is prepared and added to the clarified juice at 3% by volume. Since we have already discussed the preparation of such a starter, we will not elaborate further here.

Recommended fermentation temperatures for white wines are from 55-65° F. Because of their delicate nature, fermentation at higher temperatures may produce a variety of unpleasant characters that become obvious in the finished wine. Large-scale fermentations, unless controlled, will theoretically exhibit a temperature increase of 2.3° F. for every 1° Balling lost in the conversion of sugar to alcohol. If unchecked this temperature increase would soon kill the yeasts, resulting in what is called a "stuck" fermentation. Industrially, the problem of temperature control is remedied by pumping the fermenting juice through specially designed heat-exchange equipment at regular intervals. We have found, however, that heat transfer and dissipation is generally not a problem in fermentation volumes of less than 25 gallons held at a relatively constant ambient temperature. If you do happen to note an increase in the temperature of your fermentations you might consider setting the fermenter in a tub of cold water. In five- to ten-gallon lots, this will likely as not stabilize the temperature increase and prevent further problems.[2]

Post-Fermentation Processing: Careful and continuous racking is the key to producing a sound wine at this point. As a rule of thumb, you may expect the majority of lees to be removed in three thorough rackings. However, continue to observe the progress of clarification and rack as sediment collects. Remember that any headspace left in storage containers serves to initiate chemical oxidation as well as possible microbial spoilage. Liberal use of nitrogen gas to purge oxygen from empty containers prior to filling and "topping off" partially filled containers is advised.

Sweet Table Wine Production: Special attention should be given, at this point, to production of slightly sweet table wine. Currently, white wines having 1-2% residual sugar are very sought-after products. Among winemakers, there are several methods employed in production of slightly sweet wines, depending upon their available technology. If the plant has a means of high-speed separation of solids, the wine may be clarified, and fermentation stopped at any point in the process. The equipment needed, however, is in some cases prohibitively expensive. Although the wines produced by this method are generally regarded as being superior to those made by other methods, cost and, in some cases, available expertise for operation, may block this avenue.

A second commonly used method involves the addition of approximately 0.060 grams per liter of sulfur dioxide to the fermentation and lowering the temperature to less than 30° F. This method, when applied to lots of less than five gallons, is not beyond the means of the home vintner. It will involve storage in a refrigerator-freezer during the clarification process. In lots larger than five gallons, the cooling capacity of the average refrigerator may not be sufficient to effect cessation of full fermentation. In these cases, we recommend apportioning the volume into several one-gallon containers, adding the SO_2 , and then storing in the cold box.

The third, and recommended, method for the home operation is simply to allow the wine to ferment to dryness and sweeten with white grape concentrate at a latter stage, usually just prior to bottling. Although wines produced by this method may, in the opinion of some, lack much of the fruity nature characteristic of the first two procedures, they may nevertheless be quite pleasant. This method has the added advantage of not requiring special refrigeration equipment during most of the processing.

Oak Aging of White Wines: Generally speaking, the home vintner should not attempt aging of white wine in oak. However, some white varieties, namely Chardonnay and Johannesberg Riesling, may merit from a brief exposure to wood. If you decide to attempt oak aging, do so with a great deal of care. Pay special attention to overexposure that can develop from prolonged storage. In new cooperage, this is a major consideration in that the first vintage stored in the wood will extract much of the oak character in a shorter-than-expected period. Another problem area, especially in new cooperage, is "fill levels." Even though the barrel may be tightly bunged, evaporation of the wine through pores in the wood will result in a head-space developing around the bung. This should be checked at bi-weekly intervals and filled or "topped" as necessary. Use of barrel wax around the bung may help in preventing some of this loss. In short, we feel

that for the home operation, barrel aging is best re-
served for red wines where defects in cooperage or
technique are less apparent.

Bottling: When you feel that your wine is ready for
bottling, proceed as in the case of fruit wines. A sulfur
dioxide addition of 0.030 grams per liter is recommended (see Equation 1) prior to bottling. Also, if you
are planning to bottle a sweet wine, a sorbic acid addition of 0.350 grams per liter should be made according to Equation 4. As a general rule, white wines should
be aged at least six to eight weeks before opening.

The Blanc d'Noir Style Wines

Although the practice is quite old, use of certain red
grape varieties to produce white wine has recently
received some attention among American vintners.
Some winemakers feel that white wines vinified in this
manner are heavier in body and character than those
produced from traditional white varieties. The winemaker should take care to select only those red varieties that are naturally low in color. This obviously
precludes use of Teinturier varieties, with pink-red
flesh. In addition to the traditional Pinot Noir used
in French Champagnes, we recommend Barbera or
Grenache. Additionally, some cellars are marketing
Zinfandel produced in this style.

Grapes for this purpose should be harvested in early
season before full maturity. At harvest, extra care must
be taken to prevent damage to the grape. Moldy and
defective berries and clusters should be excised. As in

the traditional style of the French, grapes should be gently pressed, not crushed. Crushing releases skin pigments that will contribute to excess unwanted color. At pressing, a sulfur dioxide addition should be made at a level of 0.060 grams per kilogram of fresh fruit. It is suggested that this solution be incorporated into the grapes and juice. The juice is then collected into nitrogen-sparged carboys and held under refrigeration overnight for clarification. The next morning, juice is racked free of lees, the appropriate volume of yeast starter added, and fermentation initiated at 55-60° F. Since grapes used in this winemaking style are less mature than normal, hence higher in acid, there is usually no need to adjust the acidity of the juice. Wines produced in this manner are best fermented to dryness utilizing the same processing mode as described for other white varieties.

After clarification, one will note that the wine will have a copper to pinkish hue. Although this is to be expected, you may wish to reduce or eliminate this excessive color by use of decolorizing charcoal. Since the applications of charcoal are considered under the topic of "fining," we will only mention at this point that this agent is very effective in removing unwanted color from a wine.

Red Table Wines

Crushing and Fermentation: With the exception of certain varieties with pigmented pulp, the color in red wines is attributed to contact time with the grape skins during active fermentation. Although the fermentation process, itself, extracts a majority of the color, enhanced color may be achieved by use of slightly higher levels of sulfur dioxide at crush. Thus, in the production of red wines, it is common practice to add 0.100 grams of sulfur dioxide per kilogram of fresh grapes. In the form of metabisulfite, this amounts to 9 grams per 100 pounds of grapes. Following crush, an active yeast starter is added at 3% of the total volume and fermentation allowed to proceed at temperatures from 75-80° F. Since wine pigment is extracted from the skins, it is necessary to frequently mix the "cap," consisting of skins and pulp that rises to the top due to fermentation gas, into the liquid portion of the fermentation. This process, called "punching," can be affected either by use of a wooden pole or "punch" or by hand.

Pressing: When the desired color has been developed, the cap should be removed and pressed to extract remaining soluble color and juice which may have been retained in the skins. Generally speaking, pressing of a dry red wine takes place around 7° Balling, although this will vary depending upon the winemaker. Rosés, by comparison, are produced by pressing at an earlier time, usually 12-14° Balling. Since the color of a rosé is somewhat variety dependent, experience alone is often the basis of the winemaker's decision on pressing time. At pressing, free-run and press lots are maintained separately for blending at a later time. After pressing, the liquid portions are returned to their containers and fermentation allowed to proceed to dryness. Again, care must be taken to prevent the entry of oxygen at this and subsequent stages.

Post Fermentation Processing: At dryness, the young wine should be given an SO_2 addition of 0.030 grams per liter according to Equation 1, and either barrelled or held for clarification prior to barrelling. We recommend the latter procedure. If you choose the former route, take care not to bung the barrel tightly until after the second racking. Trapped gases escaping from the wine may build pressure faster than they can dissipate through pores in the wood, resulting in a potential bomb! Another problem with barrel clarification is that lees become trapped between the staves, thus serving as a permanent source of nutrient for spoilage micro-organisms.

As with any wine, racking should continue until no sediment is noted. Red wines, depending upon their individual character, may be held in wood for several years. During the aging process, you should routinely check the fill level and "top off" any ullage that may have developed due to evaporation. It is always a good idea to ferment several gallons more than needed to fill your barrel. This wine can be kept in gallon containers and used as topping material. All subsequent processing is no different from that employed in white wine production. Prior to bottling, SO_2 is added at prescribed levels and, if you plan a sweetened lot, red concentrate is added at the desired level along with sorbic acid to inhibit refermentation.

4

DESSERT WINE PRODUCTION

An INTERESTING, ALTHOUGH somewhat expensive alternative to table wine is the production of dessert wines. Ports and Muscatels are treated as any fermentation except that they are arrested at an early stage by the addition of alcohol. Industrially, this is achieved by addition of fortifying alcohol, or, as it is called, "high proof." For the home operation, we recommend the use of a high quality vodka for the fortification step. *Do not* use any pharmaceutical alcohols; these are poisonous!! To add the correct amount of alcohol, it is necessary to know only the sugar content of the grapes at crush, the sugar content of the wine at the time of fortification, and the proof content of the alcohol to be added. The sugar contents are obtained by use of a hydrometer and the alcohol proof is printed on the label. Commercially available vodkas range from 80 to 100° proof. Since one percent alcohol is equivalent to two degrees proof, the alcohol content varies from 45-50% by volume. The difference in sugar content before crush and fortification divided by two yields the alcohol present in the wine before fortification. With this information you can use the simplified formula presented on the following page to calculate the quantity of vodka to add to yield a wine of 20% alcohol by volume.

Equation 5:[3]

Alcohol Additions (in gallons) =

$$\frac{\text{desired alcohol} - \text{alcohol present at fortification}}{\text{\% alcohol of vodka added} - \text{desired alcohol level in finished product}} \times \text{gallons of wine}$$

Assuming one gallon of actively fermenting wine with an initial sugar content of 24° Balling and fortification at 18° Balling with 90° proof vodka, we may calculate the addition using Equation 5:

$$\text{Alcohol Addition (in gallons)} = \frac{20\% - 3\%}{45\% - 20\%} \times 1 \text{ gallon} = 0.76 \text{ gallon}$$

Port Processing

As a red dessert wine of approximately 20% alcohol, a vintage port may become one of the most prized wines in the cellar. Ports, as a class, have the capability of aging for years, being relatively insensitive to the problems of old age. As a young wine of intense color and character, the designation "ruby" is applied. With advanced age, however, most ports deposit some of their pigment as a sediment that may cover the sides of the bottle. With the onset of brownish overtones, associated with maturity, the port is referred to as being "tawney." Practically speaking, not all ports marketed today under the designation "tawney" are old. In our discussion of aging of muscatels and sherries, we will suggest alternatives to the lengthy process of aging. These same alternatives apply equally well for port. Application of heat, for example, will produce a tawney port in a fraction of the time required by wood aging at cellar temperatures. However, only time can produce a great wine and utilization of these tricks to induce rapid aging effects may be expected to produce an inferior product.

Several grape varieties lend themselves to production as ports. These include Tinta Madiera, Tinta Cao, Souzao, and Royalty. Other table wine varieties that occasionally find their way into ports include Zinfandel, Ruby Cabernet and Alicante Bouschet. As we mentioned in a discussion of red table wines, color extraction is primarily the result of skin contact during fermentation. While granting that varieties such as Souzao and Royalty have pigmented juice, skin contact is still of utmost importance in creating a wine with stable color. Most port fermentations are pressed at 15-17° Balling. During this short period of fermentation, it is imperative that the cap be punched as often as possible to achieve maximum color extraction. After pressing, the calculated volume of alcohol is added to the entire volume of fermenting juice. Because of the dilution effect of vodka, however, we recommend fortification to 16-17% (v/v) alcohol. Unfortunately, fortifications to higher commercially acceptable levels may result in a wine of deficient body and character.

Since the alcohol used in fortification has a lower density than does the fermenting juice, thorough mixing is necessary to prevent stratification. Established industry standards call for an "apparent" 7° Balling, as measured by hydrometer, after fortification. In some texts you may notice the notation "20 x 7" which makes reference to the fact that at 20% alcohol, the apparent Balling reads seven.

After fortification and thorough mixing, the entire lot should be allowed to clarify. You will note the immediate large volume of lees that are deposited as compared with normal fermentations. To increase your yield, you may want to collect these lees into a second container and allow them to settle further. Upon completion of your third racking, the port should be transferred to oak for aging. Because of production costs, you may want to purchase smaller volume cooperage or utilize oak chips in the manner discussed earlier.

Muscatels

Owing to the stigma of cheap consumption that has been attached to the wine, muscatels have fallen into disrepute. Although this trend, of late, shows signs of reversing, some wine experts continue to describe the product as appealing to the pedestrian palate. This is unfortunate because we believe that properly produced and aged, a muscatel stands as a distinctly unique and meritorious creation.

The majority of California muscatels are produced from Muscat of Alexandria. However, several other white varieties are also used as they become available. These include Muscat Frontignan (also known as Muscat Blanc or Muscat Canelli), Malvasia Bianca, and Orange Muscat. In addition, two red muscat varieties,

Hamburg and Aleatico, are occasionally bottled in limited amounts by certain cellars.

Muscats destined for dessert wine production are best harvested at 24-26° Balling. At this level of maturity, however, the variety tends to raisin badly. Since this may contribute to off color and flavor in the finished wine, shriveled or raisined berries should be excised before crush. Crushing is accomplished as discussed using an SO_2 addition of 0.100 gram per kilogram of fruit. Muscat is one of the white varieties that benefits from a period of skin contact after crushing. Therefore, it is recommended practice to ferment the grape 24-36 hours on the skins in order to extract the grape character before pressing. After pressing, free run and press juice are maintained separately and at 14-16° Balling, both are fortified to 16-17% alcohol according to instructions. Remember, the alcohol used in fortification has a lower density than the wine, and thorough mixing is an absolute necessity.

Premium quality muscatel should be aged in oak 3-4 years prior to bottling. However, one may speed up the operation by holding the wine at 120-140° F. for one to two months. This process, known as "baking," may produce a decidedly inferior product relative to the more traditional method.

Sherry

Sherry production may prove an interesting project for the winemaker during the off season. Unlike table wine production, sherry is an oxidative process, traditionally involving contact of the wine with oxygen. Thus, the sherry character is usually not varietal-dependent but rather is attributed to chemical and microbial changes during its formation. As such, relatively common grapes such as Thompson Seedless and Palomino are recommended for use as a sherry base.

After completion of the alcoholic fermentation, several rackings are necessary to yield a clean base wine or "shermat." It is noteworthy to mention here that the racking step may be omitted in traditional Spanish sherries. From this point, however, methodology varies with winemaking style.

"Flor Sherries": After fortification of shermat to 15% alcohol, by volume, Spanish Fino and Amontillado sherry base is racked into 130-gallon oak containers called "butts." These are filled to three-quarters capacity to allow an area for oxygen exchange and inoculated with a mixed culture of native "flor yeast." Flor yeasts differ from those you have used in table wine production. The most apparent difference is that the flor yeast requires the presence of oxygen for growth and conversion of alcohol to acetaldehyde, the chemical we associate with sherry character. Within several weeks, the flor forms as a layer on the surface of the young sherry. Over a period of months, some of the flor may break up, falling to the bottom to accumulate as lees. As the seasons change so does the character of the flor. During the spring, it is present as an almost continuous layer on the surface. With warmer weather, the cake breaks up and sinks, only to reform in fall and winter. Thus, you should not be con-

cerned by the presence of sediment. In fact, some reports indicate that Spanish vintners may not clean cooperage for several years, feeling that much of the sherry character is derived from the lees. Because of the time involved and the ever present problem of contamination of table wines with flor yeasts, many American producers perfer to use the alternative baking process.

"Baked Sherries": As in fino production, shermat used in baked sherries is first fortified to 15% alcohol to inhibit the growth of the vinegar bacteria, *Acetobacter*. A very close approximation of the final alcohol content of shermat may be obtained by multiplying the initial fermentable sugar content of the grape by 0.55. Then, by application of Equation 5, the necessary quantity of alcohol may be obtained. The best baked sherries begin with 1-2% sugar which is added as white grape concentrate prior to the baking stage. After thorough mixing of wine, concentrate, and alcohol, the shermat is barrelled and stored at 120-140° F. for six to eight weeks to allow for baking. When the desired effects have been achieved, the wine is returned to normal cellar temperatures for continued aging. The entire process takes less than six months from crush to bottling the finished sherry. It is generally agreed, however, that the product is inferior to the traditional Spanish method involving years of aging.

5

FINING AND
FINING AGENTS

FROM TIME TO TIME, the amateur as well as the professional winemaker may find it necessary to modify the character of his wine in order to achieve a more acceptable balance. This may involve removal of unstable protein, in the case of white wines, softening of excessive tannin levels in reds (and occasionally in whites), or reduction of oxidation pigments which have developed due to poor cellar practices. All of these come under the general topic of fining which may be operationally defined as the removal or modification of certain undesirable components from a wine in order to improve its appearance and/or organoleptic qualities. The process may or may not be selective, depending upon the agent(s) used.

Routinely, a winery may utilize several fining agents in the final preparation of its products for market. The home winemaker may find it necessary to employ one or more of these. Remember, however, deposition of materials other than yeast and fermentation debris is considered by many to be a natural phenomenon contributing to the overall character of the wine. As evidence, we find the phrase "unfiltered and unfined" on a growing number of labels from premium wineries. With this in mind, a brief discussion of available fining agents and their individual applications is presented.

Bentonite: Upon storage at cellar temperatures, most

white wines, unless specially treated, deposit a portion of their protein as a grayish-white precipitate in the bottom of the bottle. Bentonite, also known as "Wyoming clay," reconstituted as a 5% solution is very effective in the removal of these naturally occurring proteins. In that many consumers regard protein deposition as a flaw, wineries prefer to alleviate the problem before bottling by the addition of bentonite.

If you plan to produce a white wine and are concerned with possible protein deposition, it is suggested that the bentonite solution be prepared several weeks in advance and stored for "curing." Bentonite normally is prepared as a 5% solution in very hot water. Since the clay has a tendency to form lumps, which decrease its effectiveness, we recommend that the calculated amount be added slowly to the water with thorough mixing. You may find it necessary to use a flour sifter to create a uniform powder for addition. The resultant mixture should be homogenous in appearance.

It is normal practice for the winemaker first to establish to what degree proteins will present a problem in the wine. Routinely, this determination is made by use of the so-called "pan test," which simply involves heating a few ounces of the wine to near boiling and observing the quantity of precipitate which forms the following day. Experience alone is the best guide in evaluation of the results and determining the quantity of fining agent needed to achieve stability.

Depending upon grape variety and the area from which it came, the quantity of bentonite required may range from the equivalent of one pound per thousand gallons upward to the equivalent of 5-6 pounds per thousand gallons. After establishing the presence of protein instability, the winemaker normally establishes the minimum quantity of fining agent needed to remedy the problem. This is accomplished by collection of measured amounts of wine into three sample jars. The equivalent of one pound per thousand gallons is added to the first, two pounds to the second, and so forth. Each is then shaken thoroughly to disperse the agent and allowed to settle at room temperature. When clear, a few ounces from each are drawn into separate containers and a second set of pan tests carried out. By comparison to the untreated sample run earlier, the winemaker is then able to determine the minimum quantity needed to achieve stability. This amount is then added to the total wine lot according to Table 1:

Table 1

Equivalent weight per thousand gallons	Volume of 5% solution per 10 gallons of wine	
	Metric measure (milliliters)	English measure (ounces)
1 pound	97.6 ml	3.3 oz.
2 pounds	192.2 ml	6.5 oz.
3 pounds	289.8 ml	9.8 oz.
4 pounds	384.4 ml	13.0 oz.
5 pounds	482.0 ml	16.3 oz.
6 pounds	591.46 ml	20.0 oz.

Usually, 3-4 days are needed for the bentonite to settle from solution. At this time, the wine should be carefully racked from its lees. You will probably note that bentonite does not form compact lees and that some may be carried over, thus necessitating a second racking. It is essential that the wine not be allowed to remain in contact with bentonite for prolonged periods. Such a practice imparts an earthy taste to the wine.

Red wines normally do not exhibit protein instability. The naturally occurring proteins form complexes with wine tannins. Because of increased molecular weight and insolubility, these complexes then precipitate from solution. A word of caution should be included here. The addition of bentonite to young red wines will result in loss of significant amounts of color.

Charcoal: The importance of charcoal as an effective decolorizing and deodorizing agent in wine has been recognized for hundreds of years. One common application is in the removal of brown oxidation pigments that develop in improperly treated wines. Another use is in removal of excess color as discussed under the topic of Blanc d'Noir style wines. Additionally, certain malodors may be decreased or eliminated by use of this fining agent. Although the addition level varies as to the nature of the problem, the equivalent of one pound per thousand gallons may be achieved by adding 0.16 ounces per ten gallons of wine. Carbon particles frequently remain in solution and are difficult to remove. Therefore, it is often necessary to follow a "carbon fining" with the addition of bentonite at equivalent levels of 1-2 pounds per thousand gallons.

Please note that while charcoal is efficient in reducing or eliminating browning in a wine, excessive amounts will strip it of much of its vinous nature. Therefore, we suggest careful testing prior to addition to your wine.

Egg White Fining: Egg albumen finds its greatest popularity among European winemakers who use it to soften overly astringent red and white wines. While egg albumen is not utilized extensively among American winemakers, those who use it recommend 1-2 whites per fifty gallons of wine. If you plan to experiment with this fining agent, we suggest that the whites be beaten thoroughly in a blender and mixed with approximately one gallon of wine and then added into the total lot.

Gelatin Fining: We have saved this agent for last because of its potential for causing problems. Made from highly refined bone, gelatin is reconstituted in warm water as a 0.5% solution. The latter is then added to the wine according to Table 2.

Table 2

Equivalent weight per thousand gallons	Volume of 0.5% solution per gallon of wine	
	Metric measure (milliliters)	English measure (ounces)
1 pound	91.7 ml	3.1 oz.
2 pounds	183.4 ml	6.2 oz.
3 pounds	272.1 ml	9.2 oz.

In wine, gelatin absorbs several times its own weight and as such, is very effective in removal of tannins in both red and white wines. In California, gelatin finds its most common application in white wines. The danger here, however, is one of over-addition. After reaction with wine tannins, gelatin remaining in the wine forms a haze which is difficult to remove. If such a problem is encountered, it may be corrected by addition of bentonite at the equivalent weight of one pound per thousand gallons. However, in addition to the extra time and material needed in counter-fining, there will also be losses owing to the voluminous nature of bentonite lees. Therefore, if you plan to use this fining agent, care should be taken to run several trials to establish minimum levels for addition to the finished wine.

6

WINE MICROBIOLOGY

W<small>E FREQUENTLY RECEIVE CALLS</small> from home winemakers regarding the poor quality of their wine and how to correct the problem. Others simply ask if their slightly defective product is safe to drink. In some cases the problem(s) are non-microbial in nature. It is hoped that the first several chapters will provide an insight into corrections needed in these areas. However, many times the defect(s) are clearly biological and for this reason we have prepared this discussion on the bacteriological considerations of winemaking.

First of all we would like to lay to rest the question "is my wine safe to drink?" Assuming that no toxic chemicals have come into contact with either grape or wine, the answer is yes. Wine is reported to be "the most hygienic of all beverages," in that no human pathogens are known to survive in it. In fact, this is one of the chief reasons that wine has been consumed for centuries. Since disease, in many cases, is water borne, man in many countries turned to wine as an alternative to water. Although a discussion of the hygienic nature of this beverage would necessarily involve a multiplicity of factors beyond the scope of this discussion, two important ones come to mind, namely wine acidity and alcohol content.

The contribution of wine acids in the inhibition of pathogenic bacteria has been recognized since the early investigations of Pasteur. Embodied in a consideration of acidity is the concept of pH, which is a measure of the availability of acidic groups. The logarithmic pH scale runs from 0-14, with 0-7 being acidic and 7-14 basic. Wine pH normally runs from 3.3 to slightly over 4.0. The contribution of fixed wine acids is then to maintain the pH at these low levels. Microorganisms as a group thrive within the pH range 5-8. While yeast and certain wine bacteria are insensitive to pH in the range of 3.3-4.0, pathogenic bacteria have their lower tolerance limits at a pH of 4.5. Hence, these organisms are not a problem in wine.

Of equal importance in microbial inhibition is the role of alcohol content. Although the alcohol level of a dry table wine is not sufficient to inhibit growth of wine spoilage organisms such as acetic and lactic acid bacteria, it is more than sufficient to prevent the growth of any pathogenic microbe. Also of importance is the role of sulfur dioxide that is added at several steps in the processing of grapes into wine. At the usual levels of 0.075-0.150 grams per liter, SO_2 is efficient not only in inhibiting pathogens but also wine spoilage organisms. We should point out here that while each of these parameters may be effective in itself at inhibition of pathogens, they act together, in conjunction with many other factors, to make wine truly the most hygienic of beverages. With this brief introduction into wine microbiology, let us move on into a discussion of some of the important wine microorganisms and the problems they produce.

Acetification and Acetobacter: Based on several

years of experience with homemade wines, it is safe to say that the most commonly encountered microbial problem is acetification. Also known as "vinegar souring" or "volatile acidity," this form of spoilage is the result of an aerobic bacterial conversion of alcohol to acetic acid. The micro-organisms involved may belong to several species of *Acetobacter*, the most commonly reported being *Acetobacter oxydans* and *Acetobacter aceti*. The acetic acid content is commonly used as an index of wine quality. At the production level, California law prohibits the sale of red or white table wine with an acetic acid content of more than 0.120 and 0.110 grams per 100 ml respectively. Actually, the average person can detect the presence of this acid at levels of approximately 0.08 grams per 100 ml.

While it is impossible, under normal conditions, to control the occurrence of this ubiquitous bacteria, the winemaker can prevent its growth. An important key in the control of *Acetobacter* is oxygen contact. Since this microbe requires oxygen for growth and reproduction, care should be taken to minimize oxygen contact with the wine.

Although normally associated with improper storage of wines, the volatile acid content of a red wine may originate in the cap during the later stages of fermentation. During this period, gaseous evolution is not sufficient to prevent entrance of oxygen and growth of *Acetobacter*. For this reason we have stressed the importance of pressing the cap at 7° Balling while the fermentation is still proceeding strongly. Normally, increases in volatile acidity occur during the aging process. Therefore, wines stored in oak cooperage should be routinely checked for fill levels and topped as necessary. If you have glass or stainless steel storage, routine use of nitrogen gas in addition to a tight seal is adequate for protection of wines in partially filled containers. Where glass carboys are used, an effective seal may be achieved by use of polyethylene sandwich wraps sold at the market. We have found that wines stored under these conditions will hold for months without change. In conjunction with maintaining wine under minimal oxygen conditions, sulfur dioxide is very effective in inhibiting bacterial growth. Use of SO_2 as discussed in earlier sections, is additional "insurance" against potential problems.

Owing largely to available technology, industrial encounters with acetification problems are limited largely to isolated occurrences. Large-scale use of stainless steel tanks coupled with careful and continued monitoring of wines in storage have reduced the role of this spoilage organism to that of historical interest.

The Malolactic Fermentation: Generally speaking, the lactic acid bacteria present a greater economic challenge to the professional winemaker than do their close relatives, the acetic acid bacteria. During their growth stages, micro-organisms in this group enzymatically convert the malic acid present in the wine to lactic acid and two or more byproducts. Included in the latter are the compounds diacetyl and acetoin which are reported to contribute to wine complexity. Also, depending upon the bacteria involved, carbon dioxide gas may be evolved as part of the reaction series. The result of the malolactic fermentation is reduction in wine acidity. In some cases, this may result in loss of up to one-third of the total acid content. Furthermore, growth of some lactic organisms, especially the lactobacilli, is said to impart a "mousey" character to the wine.

Whether the winemaker considers the malolactic fermentation as a spoilage situation depends largely upon the initial acidity of the grapes. For example, grapes grown in northern climates may have such a high initial acid content that the final wine may be unpalatable. In these instances, the winemaker may elect to encourage the bacterial fermentation. As an example, the great red wines of Bordeaux and Burgundy attribute much of their character to the malolactic fermentation. At present, some premium California wineries are inducing the fermentation, in the later stages of alcoholic fermentation, using specially selected lactic strains. By comparison to cooler regions, grapes harvested in warmer areas such as the San Joaquin Valley of California, are normally of average or deficient acidity. Any subsequent reduction in acid content produces a wine of little character. Thus, winemakers from these areas tend to discourage the fermentation.

As compared with *Acetobacter*, the three genera of lactic acid bacteria, *Leuconostoc*, *Lactobacillus*, and *Pediococcus*, grow only under conditions where oxygen is limiting. Thus, if not controlled, the fermentation may begin once the wine has been bottled. At this stage, the product will become turbid and throw a heavy sediment. Additionally, gas formation will leave the wine with a "spritzy" sensation and, if formed in sufficient volumes, push corks. The result is obvious spoilage.

Several methods are employed in prevention of the malolactic fermentation. At the home level, the best method is continued and thorough racking as lees appear. Remember, lees serve as an excellent source of nutrient, especially vitamins, for bacterial growth and their removal, obviously, deprives the microorganism of this source. Secondly, maintenance of adequate sulfur dioxide levels, usually 0.100 to 0.125 grams per liter, is a necessity in control. As a final suggestion, storage of the product at refrigeration temperatures is useful when used in conjunction with the first two procedures.

A final very important note regarding lactic acid bacteria is needed here. These microbes are capable of breaking down sorbic acid, the end product of which is an ether-like compound strongly reminiscent of geraniums. Therefore, if you plan to use sorbic acid to stablilize a sweet table wine for bottling, special care must be taken either to insure that the malolactic fermentation does not occur, or that it has occurred prior to the sorbic acid addition. We suggest, for the serious winemaker, purchase of supplies needed to monitor the occurrence of bacterial fermentation. The procedure involves a simple chromatographic separation that may be carried out in a mayonnaise jar according to established procedures. Chemicals and supplies may be purchased through winery supply outlets.

"Wine Flowers" and Candida mycoderma: This occasionally troublesome yeast may be found growing at the surface of low alcohol wines which are exposed to the air. Its presence can be recognized by development of a thin whitish film referred to as "wine flowers." Also known as "film yeasts," *Candida* causes oxidation of alcohol and wine acids resulting in a defective product frequently exhibiting an aldehydic character. As with *Acetobacter* spoilage, the problem is best prevented by restricting oxygen contact with the wine. If you happen to note a film forming, the addition of sulfur dioxide at 0.030 grams per liter will usually take care of the problem. Also, check the seal and top with nitrogen to purge any oxygen within the container's volume.

In certain cases, namely improperly stabilized sweet wines, wine yeasts themselves may bring about refermentation and spoilage. The reader is referred to earlier discussions on the use of sorbic acid as an inhibitor of yeast growth.

Mold Growth on Cooperage: Several species of mold are commonly found growing on wine barrels, especially during winter months when humidity is generally high. While fungistatic preparations are available for coating barrels, sanitation may prove to be the real key. Check for leaks that may have developed in your barrels. Also, wine should not be allowed to accumulate in puddles beneath barrels. These serve as excellent sites for mold growth. Any mold growth around the bung may be stopped by impregnating the wax seal with potassium metabisulfite. However, if all else fails, the fact that these molds require oxygen for growth will prevent them from ending up in your wine!

7

SENSORY
EVALUATION

Hᴏᴡ ɪs ᴍʏ ᴡɪɴᴇ ᴅᴇᴠᴇʟᴏᴘɪɴɢ? What are its strengths, its weaknesses, its potential? These are questions that professional winemakers must ask themselves on a daily basis. The answers to these and other questions then serve to dictate future blending, bottling, and sales considerations. Thus, careful objective evaluation of the maturing wine is as important to the success of an operation as any step in the processing line. In like manner, the amateur enologist should routinely monitor the progress of his product. To the novice, wine appraisal, technically referred to as "organoleptic evaluation," may seem, at best, pretentious. However, with experience and time, one can gain a measure of facility with the art.

The "tools of the trade," so to speak, are relatively inexpensive: an 8-ounce clear wine glass and reasonably functioning visual, olfactory and gustatory systems. Additionally, one will probably want to utilize some sort of score card for record keeping. While several methods of rating wines have been developed, we recommend the 20-point scale shown on page 88. The available 20 points are divided into ten categories, each weighted as to its overall importance in wine quality. Since you will undoubtedly want to retain information for future reference, it is suggested that score cards be prepared on 8½ x 11″ paper for easy filing in either notebooks or binders. A common flaw of many rating cards is lack of available space for comments. Since impressions and notations are invaluable, many tasting groups and winemakers choose to modify score sheets to allow for more space after each category. We prefer at least twice the area available on the sample card included in this book.

Largely for continuity, most scoring systems are set up to test the logical course of events in the total spectrum of perception. Thus, we first consider the visual attributes, followed by aromatic or olfactory sensations, and concluding with taste and tactile responses. Accordingly, the sample score card begins with the considerations of appearance and color, followed by the olfactory categories of aroma, bouquet and acescence, and ending with the gustatory sensations of acidity, sugar, and flavor. The categories of body and astringency are largely tactile responses that tend to modify the character and quality of the wine on one's palate response. A final consideration on this card is general quality, which allows the judge a final opportunity to express himself. As a result, we often find that this category is the most subjective portion of the evaluation. Regardless of numerical scores applied to each category, the most useful information comes from careful notations made during tasting sessions. Remember, unless one has an excellent memory, numerical values may lose their importance with time!

In practice, judges may be as free or restrictive with points as they wish. The provision here is that they be consistent in their responses. That is, one should strive for uniform application of standards which do not vary greatly from sample to sample within any one session or between sessions. Only with uniformity can the merits or defects of one wine be compared with those of another.

SCORE CARD

Wine No. or Name						
Appearance (2)						
Color (2)						
Aroma & Bouquet (4)						
Acescence (2) (Volatile Acidity)						
Total Acid (2)						
Sugar (1)						
Body (1)						
Flavor (2)						
Astringency (2)						
General Quality (2)						
TOTAL						

17 to 20, wines must have some outstanding characteristic and no marked defect; 13 to 16, standard wines with neither an outstanding character or defect; 9 to 12, wines of commercial acceptability but with a noticeable defect; 5 to 8, wines of below commercial acceptability; 1 to 4, completely spoiled wines.

Sample score sheet as used in the Departments of Enology at California State University, Fresno, and the University of California at Davis.

8

SPARKLING WINE PRODUCTS

"Come quickly brothers, I am drinking stars."
Dom Perignon, c. 1680

THE CHANCE DISCOVERY of refermentation by Dom Pierre Perignon in 1680 launched what has become one of the most successful and glamorous areas in the field of winemaking. As testimony to the importance of his discovery, one of France's finest Champagnes bears his name. The current popularity of Champagne is indicated in a recent article in *Food and Wine Magazine* (December 1981) where a representative of the French firm of Moët et Chandon proudly points out, "throughout the world, a Moët cork flies every 1.7 seconds."

Since the carbonation discovered by Perignon was certainly not planned, we can speculate on its likely sources. Although there are other possibilities, two come to mind immediately: (1) refermentation, and (2) bacterial malolactic fermentation. In the first case, one could propose that an early, cold winter (not unexpected given the northerly latitude of Hautvilliers, France) arrested a slowly fermenting wine before its completion. Upon clarification during the winter months, the winemaker may have, unknowingly, bottled the wine with residual fermentable sugar. With the first warm days of spring, yeasts remaining in the wine began to slowly ferment the sugar to produce the effervescent product. Another potential source of Dom Perignon's bubbles could have been the growth of malolactic bacteria in the bottled wine. These bacteria convert malic acid, present in the wine, to lactic acid and carbon dioxide gas. Since these organisms grow best under conditions where oxygen is limited, a bottled wine (with unutilized malic acid) is a near-perfect environment for their growth.

In either case, the ebullient beverage quickly grew in popularity. Because early-day Champagne workers lacked the expertise necessary to produce a product of consistent quality, the fruits of their labor graced only the tables of the wealthy. However, with developing technology, sparkling wine is now available to most consumers at a price generally commensurate with the effort expended in producing it. The latter qualifying comment is needed to explain the variation in prices one observes for seemingly the same product. A trip to the wine shop will quickly reveal that sparkling wine can range from as little as $2 a bottle to well over $50. To the neo-oenophile, the reasons for this apparent disparity in price may not be immediately obvious. The next few pages will serve to clarify the situation.

Intentional carbonation of wine may be accomplished in several ways. Certain table wine types may merit from a hint of carbonation (*pétillance*). Provided the gassiness does not exceed the governmentally imposed limit of 1 atmosphere of pressure, these wines are not subject to the sparkling wine tax of $3.40 per wine gallon. Such wines are carbonated at bottling by injection of carbon dioxide gas into the bottling tank or lines leading to the bottler. By comparison to the pétillant style of table wine, sparkling wine production actually involves the fermentative action of yeast. The conversion of sugar to alcohol and carbon dioxide is accomplished in a closed container such that the gas is not lost to the atmosphere. Modern-day sparkling wines may be produced in three ways.

(1) *The Charmat ("Bulk Process") Method:* Many of the inexpensive American sparkling wines are produced by this technique. In this case, the still base wine intended for refermentation is put into large tanks designed to withstand pressure differences caused by the production of CO_2 in a closed container. To the wine base, a calculated amount of sugar needed to yield 4–5 atmospheres (60–80 lbs/inch^2) of pressure, upon complete fermentation, is added and the contents thoroughly mixed. A yeast starter is added, and the tank sealed. The cuvée, as it is now called, is allowed to undergo fermentation at controlled temperatures. The period of fermentation depends upon temperature and usually takes 2–3 weeks. Upon completion of fermentation, the wine is clarified, filtered, and bottled. Transferring the wine from one container at near 80 psi, through a filter, to a second tank presents interesting technical problems. In order not to lose the carbonation, the entire process must be done at constant pressure. Therefore, a counter pressure, equal to that in the fermentation tank, must be applied to the receiving tank, filter and the lines connecting each. Transfer and filtration can then be accomplished without product loss. Normally, Charmat-style sparkling wines are not aged for extended periods before being shipped to retail outlets.

Sparkling wines produced by the Charmat method

are typically, but not always, closed with a polyethylene closure, thus significantly shortening their aging capacity. We are, however, aware of one California producer of Charmat-style sparkling wines that not only uses a traditional Champagne cork closure, but also uses the heavier bottle-fermented Champagne bottle, complete with a punt in the bottom. In this case, the product resembles, in all respects, most of the bottle-fermented sparkling wines of California. However, by law, wines produced using the Charmat-technique, must state on the label: "Charmat," or "Bulk Process."

The United States government defines "Champagne" as being produced in closed containers of less than 1 gallon capacity. The next two production techniques fit this definition. In both cases, the sparkling wines are bottle-fermented and differ principally in the method of sediment removal once the secondary fermentation has been completed. Sparkling wines produced in these styles generally state on the bottle "Bottle Fermented," or "Naturally Fermented in *The* Bottle," or "Naturally Fermented in *This* Bottle," but such information is only voluntary.

(2) *The Transfer Method:* In this style of sparkling wine, the sugared and yeasted cuvée is put into individual heavy-duty bottles. The contents are sealed with a crown cap closure, the bottles are laid on their sides, and the refermentation occurs in the bottle. Upon completion of secondary fermentation and aging (if any), each bottle is opened and the contents transferred to a pressurized tank. The sparkling wine is then

filtered and rebottled. Such wines may state on the label "Bottle Fermented," or "Naturally Fermented in *The* Bottle."

(3) *"La Methode Champenoise"*: Without question, the world's finest sparkling wines are produced using this technique—never leaving the bottle in which they were born. As in the transfer method, the cuvée is sugared to yield a defined final pressure of carbon dioxide, yeasted, and put into the bottles. The bottles are closed with crown caps, laid on their sides, and the fermentation allowed to occur. The secondary fermentation may take up to 6 months, or longer, depending upon temperature, yeast strain, etc. Once complete, the wines are allowed to remain in contact with their lees for 1–4 years. With respect to aging on the lees, French Champagne must have at least one year's contact time to qualify for the appellation "Vin de Champagne." During aging, the sediment must occassionally be broken up to prevent permanent deposition ("masking") on the sides of the bottle. The sediment is eventually removed by gravity clarification; that is, the wines are placed, neck down, on A-frame racks called "riddling pits." At regular intervals, the bottles are turned a quarter of a turn, causing the sediment to slide down the sides and eventually lodge firmly against the closure. The process, called *remuage* or, more simply, riddling, may take several weeks for completion. A single *remueur* (riddler) can, reportedly, turn from 25,000 to 30,000 bottles in a single day. Obviously, this is a labor-intensive process, and several California cellars have sought to automate this step by construct-

ing large riddling pits on rollers. At regular intervals, the entire pit shifts, thereby simulating the effect of turning by hand. In the opinion of many, however, the traditional method of hand turning produces the best clarity.

The next step is to remove the sediment from the bottle. This step, called *degorgement* or disgorging, calls for the pre-chilled bottles to be placed neck down into an ice brine. After a short period, the volume in the first ½ inch of the neck freezes. With the sediment firmly encased in ice, the crown cap is removed with a special tool resembling a bottle opener. The pressure inside pushes the ice plug gently (or sometimes not so gently if the bottles were not cold enough) from the bottle. The bottle and its sparkling clear contents are then returned to the upright position (for the first time in over a year) and the fill-level adjusted with aged still base wine to which has been added sufficient cognac or brandy such that the final alcohol content of the new sparkling wine is near 12% (v/v). Each bottle is then quickly closed to prevent loss of carbonation and contents. Although Champagne connoisseurs frequently prefer the naturally dry style, many cellars choose to sweeten the final product in an effort to appeal to larger numbers of consumers. In this case the dosage is prepared as a sugar-syrup in the wine base and brandy and added to each bottle at the prescribed amount to yield the desired sweetness level. Thus, the consumer has a range of sweetness levels from which to choose:

Terminology   Expected Sweetness Level
Natural (Natur) .....no sugar added
Brut 0.1-1.0%
Extra Sec...........1.0-2.0%
Sec 2.0-4.0%
Demi-Sec 4.0-6.0%
Doux ....6.0% or more

For reasons that must seem obvious by this point, the home Champagne master is limited to the Methode Champenoise. The remainder of this chapter will describe how to produce sparkling wine using this method.

Producing a sound sparkling wine is not difficult given some instruction. Further, the process requires relatively little in the way of special equipment, with two important exceptions. There is an absolute requirement for (1) a full-face shield, and (2) heavy gloves. Remember, you will be handling pressurized glass bottles (70–80 psi), and there is the ever-present possibility of an explosion. While cuts can be sutured and, eventually, heal, a new eye is difficult to obtain!!

Grape Selection: As with most successful endeavors, quality sparkling wine production requires planning. The first concern must be the grapes used for the cuvée. The often-quoted adage "You can't make good wine from bad grapes ... " could not be more true in the case of sparkling wine fermentations. Not only must the fruit be absolutely sound (free from insect and mold damage) at harvest, but there are additional considerations that must be kept in mind when de-

ciding on a crush date. Two of the most important of
these concerns are sugar and acidity.

Grapes destined for sparkling wine cuvée are harvested in early season, generally before 21–22° Balling.
This is to insure that the still base wine used for cuvée
have from 10.5–11.5% (v/v) alcohol upon complete
fermentation. Since the secondary (sparkling wine)
fermentation places potentially severe metabolic stress
on the yeast, cuvée alcohol levels of more than 12% must
be avoided. Conversely, alcohol levels of less than
10.5% frequently yield sparkling wines which quickly
lose their effervescence upon opening. Early harvest
grapes are also normally higher in acidity than they
would be if harvested at more mature levels. Generally,
the acidity of sparkling wine cuvées should be at least
0.70 g/100ml and frequently higher. Where cuvées may
be deficient in natural acidity, it may be necessary to
add acids as described on page 19.

While the casual Champagne taster may not realize
it, most French Champagnes are careful blends of the
red grape variety, Pinot Noir, and the white variety,
Chardonnay. In fact, more red than white grapes find
their way into Champagne. Although Champagne
producers speak of the "heavier nose and body" of
Pinot Noir, the seemingly disproportionate amounts of
Pinot Noir and Chardonnay in French Champagne
may reflect the relative plantings of each grape. Approximately 80% of the Champagne region is planted to
Pinot Noir, with the balance as Chardonnay. If you
wish to produce sparkling wine using Pinot Noir or
other grape varieties, you would be advised to review

the processing protocol for Blanc de Noirs presented on page 51. Because Pinot Noir may prove difficult to work with, you may wish to try other red varieties. These may include Zinfandel, Barbera, and perhaps, Grenache. Remember, these varieties should be harvested early to ensure high acidity, low color, and 10.5–11.5% final alcohol upon completion of the primary fermentation.

Where the white grape variety, Chardonnay, represents the sole component in Champagne, such wine is entitled to the designation "Blanc de Blancs." This style is also seen in several of the sparkling wine cellars of California. Other white grape varieties that are frequently used in the less expensive Charmat and Transfer methods include Chenin Blanc, French Colombard, and White Riesling.

As an alternative to producing the cuvée yourself, we suggest trying an experimental lot using commercial "jug wine." Several students taking our Home Champagne Production classes have reported excellent results using such still base wines as cuvée. The important provision here is that the wine must be dry. Frequently, light sweet generic wines are stabilized with sorbic acid to prevent yeast refermentation. Obviously, such wines are of no value in production of a sparkling wine. Unfortunately, there is no easy way for the home vintner to establish whether or not the preservative has been added (such information does not appear on the label). The only suggestion we have is to purchase a bottle of potential cuvée, add some sugar and yeast to a portion, and observe what happens. If there is no activity within two days (at 60–70°F), the wine is probably not suitable for your needs. Another problem sometimes encountered, especially in "dry jug wines," is the presence of inhibitory levels of sulfur dioxide. These wines are frequently shipped from the winery soon after bottling. As a result, final SO_2 additions, made at bottling, have not had time to fully "marry" into the wine, and the level of inhibitory free SO_2 may be too high for immediate refermentation. To determine if SO_2 may be a problem, one can purchase analytical kits at most home winemaking supply shops and perform the actual analysis. Where such kits are not available, an alternative is to add 10–15 drops of 3% hydrogen peroxide (purchased at the local pharmacy) to the above sample of cuvée. If SO_2 is present at inhibitory levels, it will rapidly be converted to a noninhibitory form and the fermentation should begin in a day or so. If the problem is determined to be SO_2, the solution is simply to let the wine age in your cellar for 6–8 weeks. By this time, the levels of the compound are usually low enough for yeast to grow.

The Primary Fermentation: As with white table wine fermentations, cuvée fermentations are best done under cool conditions. For a discussion of the techniques that may be employed in cold fermentation, see pages 48–49. Since SO_2 additions may lead to partial (or complete) inhibition of the secondary fermentation, any post-fermentation additions of this compound should be limited to the smallest amount needed to prevent oxidation. Free sulfur dioxide levels at the time the cuvée is prepared, should be less than 30 ppm.

Prior to refermentation, the base wine should be properly clarified. This is best accomplished by allowing the solids to settle by gravity. If the technologist in you surfaces, and you deem a filtration necessary, use the loosest available filter pads needed to do the job. Cuvées filtered through very tight paper pads (or sterile filtered) are occasionally difficult to referment.

Commercially, several compounds may be added to the still base wine to improve its overall character prior to preparation of the cuvée. Collectively, these additives are called "fining agents" and may include bentonite, for protein stability in white wine cuvées, gelatin, to modify excessive astringency, and charcoal to reduce excess color in Blanc de Noirs. (See Chapter 5.) As we point out in Chapter 5, the addition of any compound to your wine should be limited to the minimal amount needed to accomplish your goal.

Preparation of the Cuvée

Sugar Addition (Liqueur de Cuvée): As was the case with the primary fermentation, sugar added in the secondary fermentation is converted, by the yeast, to ethanol and the desired product, carbon dioxide. Most people can recall at least one occasion when they or their parents or friends attempted to make home beer. In many cases, their efforts resulted in disaster; the bottles exploded in the cellar. At this point, the reason for the problem should be obvious: someone added too much sugar, which, through the fermentive action of the yeast, produced excessive amounts of gas which exceeded the pressure limits of the bottles. The same potential problem exists in sparkling wine production, and care must be taken in both the calculation and weighing of the correct amount of sugar to add to the still base wine. In the case of cane ("table") sugar: 4.2 grams sugar/liter = 1 atmosphere CO_2 pressure. Therefore, to prepare 5 gallons of cuvée with a potential of yielding 4 atmospheres (~60 psi) final carbonation, the calculation becomes:

Equation 6

(4.2 grams/liter) (4 atm) (5 gallons)

(3.785 liters/gallon) = *317.94 grams of table sugar*

To convert to pounds of sugar:

Equation 7

$$\frac{317.94 \text{ grams}}{454 \text{ grams/pound}} = 0.70 \text{ pounds of table sugar}$$

Obviously, any residual sugar present in the cuvée must be taken into account and subtracted from the above result. For example, if the primary fermentation stopped at 1% R.s., as determined by your Dextrocheck kit, the following correction would be necessary:

Equation 8: 1% R.s. = 1.0 grams of sugar/100 ml
of wine or 10.0 grams of sugar/liter

From the above example:

(10 grams/liter) (3.785 liters/gallon) (5 gallons)

= *189.25 grams of sugar present in still base wine*

This corrected value must be subtracted from the total weight of sugar needed to yield 4 atmospheres pressure:

317.94 grams of sugar needed

−189.25 grams of sugar present in still base wine

128.69 grams of sugar to be added

Using a glass carboy, or convenient-sized stainless steel pot from the kitchen, dissolve the calculated amount of sugar in a volume of base wine needed to effect dissolution. The syrup is then added to the total volume of base wine with thorough mixing. A yeast starter is then prepared and added (see pages 15-16). If necessary, yeast nutrient may also be added at this step. The latter, available through most home winemakers supply shops, is usually a nitrogen-based compound such as diammonium phosphate, which is sold under several proprietary labels.

Once the cuvée is prepared, it is apportioned into Champagne bottles, leaving 1-1.5″ of "head-space" in each bottle. The bottles are then sealed with a crown cap. Bottle cappers are available at prices from $5 to over $30 for the heavier-duty models. Again, a word of caution is needed here. NEVER attempt to carry out a secondary fermentation in still wine bottles. *ALWAYS* use Champagne bottles, and preferably the extra heavy-duty bottles used in the bottle-fermented style of Champagne. These are identified by their extra-heavy construction and the presence of a "punt" in the bottom.

The Secondary Fermentation: After the bottles are closed, each is laid on its side and allowed to ferment. The process may take 6 weeks, or longer, depending upon temperature. The "tirage," as this step is called, should be checked from time to time for leakers. When the fermentations begin to clarify, the fermentation has finished. If this occurs much sooner than expected, it may be necessary to carefully open a bottle to ensure that all the available sugar has been utilized.

Aging on the Lees: Upon completion of fermentation, sparkling wines are usually aged on their lees for several months (2–4 years in some French Champagnes) to enhance their flavor. Upon completion of fermentation, the bottles are carefully shaken (using face shield and gloves!) to break up the sediment. They are then laid back on their sides for aging. To prevent lees from permanently encrusting on the sides of the bottle ("masking"), this process should be repeated at 6-week intervals throughout the aging process. As a partial alternative to extensive bottle aging, we have noted that there may be some potential for aging the still base wine on its lees for several weeks at low temperature (less than 40°F.). Although our results are tentative, it appears that a yeast-like nose, not unlike that obtained by bottle aging the sparkling wine, can be obtained using the lees that accumulate after the second racking of the base wine. However, there is the possibility of developing unpleasant character if the wine is left for too long on its lees or if the temperature is allowed to increase. Therefore, this alternative should be approached with some degree of caution.

Riddling ("Remuage"): When the aging is complete, the next step is clarification. This is done by placing the bottles in a semi-inverted position and turning them 2–3 times a week or so until the sediment is concentrated against the cap. Commercially, the riddling process involves putting the bottles onto specially designed "riddling pits" that hold 120 bottles. The riddler turns

the bottles at regular intervals. Cellar workers frequently place a chalk mark across the bottom of the
bottle, and this system of "cellar bookkeeping" ensures
that all the bottles have been properly turned. Since
riddling pits are not easily acquired by home vintners,
improvisations are frequently necessary. The simplest
and most inexpensive method that we have seen is to
place the bottles neck down into a cardboard wine box.

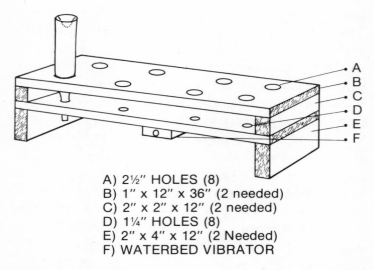

A) 2½" HOLES (8)
B) 1" x 12" x 36" (2 needed)
C) 2" x 2" x 12" (2 needed)
D) 1¼" HOLES (8)
E) 2" x 4" x 12" (2 Needed)
F) WATERBED VIBRATOR

FIGURE 9. *Schematic representation of automated riddling
pit. (Courtesy of Fred Holloway)*

Construction:
1) Position the two 1 x 12's one on top of the other.
2) Drill pilot holes.
*3) Separate boards. Using a hole saw, cut out 2½-inch holes in
    the top board and 1¼-inch holes in the bottom board.*
4) Assemble as shown in the above figure.

The bottles are then turned regularly to prevent sediment from adhering to their sides. Figure 9 shows an ingenious automated riddling pit designed by one of our former students. This design includes a water-bed vibrator to enhance the settling effect. To ensure agitation at regular intervals, a timer is included.

Removal of Sediment ("Dégorgement"): Once the sediment has firmly and completely accumulated against the crown cap closure, it is time to remove it from the bottle. The process, called disgorging or "dégorgement," involves freezing the first ½-inch of the neck in an ice brine and quickly removing the cap with a specially designed tool. In practice, a bottle opener works equally well and costs a great deal less!

Prior to disgorging, the bottles should be carefully placed in the freezer unit of the refrigerator to chill to as low a temperature as possible without actually freezing or causing the contents to "slush." The ice brine, needed to freeze the contents of the neck, is prepared as it is when one makes home ice cream: a proportionate amount of rock salt is thoroughly mixed with a bag (or more) of crushed ice. As a suggestion, an old ice chest makes a good container in which to pack the ice brine. Further, some home Champagne masters have included a wooden insert with appropriately sized holes to receive the bottles (Figure 10). An ice chest has the added advantage of being well insulated, thereby extending the life of the brine.

With face shield in place, position a bottle in the ice brine. At 2–3 minute intervals, examine the neck for development of the ice plug. When the sediment is

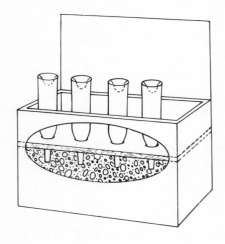

Plywood insert with
holes cut to receive
bottles.

*FIGURE 10. Degorgement bath prepared using an ice
chest,wooden insert, ice, and rock salt.*

completely encased in ice, it is time to remove the cap.
Remove the bottle from the brine and carefully wrap it
in an old towel, leaving the neck and cap exposed.
Bring the bottle to a horizontal position and, with the
bottle opener, quickly remove the cap. In a moment or
two, depending upon how much ice has formed and
how cold the bottle's contents were, the plug will begin
to slide from the bottle. Ideally, this becomes a controlled process and, with practice, even first-time
disgorgers quickly become adept at the job. It will help
the cleanup operation greatly if the bottle, and its
contents, are directed into a properly positioned receiving bucket prior to removing the closure.

Once the ice plug has been removed, speed is of the essence. Stand the bottle upright and quickly wipe down the neck and opening to remove any encrusted or accumulated debris. It is now time to adjust the fill level (and sweetness if necessary) with dosage. *Remember*, the dosage must also be ice cold. Warm dosage will cause immediate foaming and loss of much of the bottle's contents.

After the dosage has been added, insert a polyethylene Champagne closure. While there is a technique to doing this, we strongly suggest using a rubber-headed mallet to drive the closure into place. Once the closure is in place, all that remains is to place the wire hood over the closure and secure it around the bottle's neck. After disgorging, bottles should be stored on their sides, or neck down in cardboard wine boxes. Since the polyethylene closures do not effect as tight a seal as a Champagne cork closure, sparkling wines closed using these should not be expected to age well. In fact, at room temperature, the longevity of the wine may be only 6 months to one year. To prolong the life of the wine, store the bottles at refrigeration temperatures.

Preparation of the Dosage ("Liqueur d'Expédition"): About a week before you decide to disgorge, it is necessary to prepare the dosage. Dosage, in its simplest form, may consist of only aged still wine base and 4-6% brandy. If you wish to make a Brut or sweeter style of sparkling wine, it is necessary to prepare the dosage as a syrup in base wine and brandy. Since the home vintner will probably be using table sugar to prepare the dosage, it is necessary to do this ahead of time. The reason for this is that at the acidity level of wine, table sugar (a dissacharide sugar) is slowly converted to its component members. To avoid a discussion of the chemistry of sugar inversion, the bottom line, for most of us, is that there is a difference in apparent sweetness after this conversion has occurred. Therefore, if you decided that 2 tablespoons of dry table sugar per bottle was a perfect sugar level when you disgorged on December 1, you might well find that the apparent sweetness has changed when you open the bottle on New Year's Eve. This is why the dosage is prepared ahead of time: to allow this conversion to occur before bottling, such that the sweetness level you establish at bottling doesn't change with time.

Once the dosage has been prepared and aged for a week or two, it is necessary to establish the amount of alcohol-enhanced syrup to add to each bottle. This can only be done by opening a bottle and preparing a number of blends ranging from no sugar ("natural") to 2–3% or more. This is best done by measuring out several 100ml (3.5 liquid ounces) volumes of the sparkling wine into individual wine glasses. Using kitchen measuring spoons, mix different amounts of the syrup into the contents of each glass, mix well, and compare each with the others. Once the blend parameters have been established, remember to multiply the desired level by 7.5 where 750ml (1/5-gallon) bottles are used and 3.75 where 1/10-gallon bottles are used. Remember, when disgorging and adding dosage, speed is essential. Therefore, whatever final volume of dosage you decide to add, measure it into a container such that it can rapidly be added to the opened sparkling wine before the bottle's contents have a chance to warm and begin foaming.

While each Champagne cellar, no doubt, has its own "secret blend" for dosage, we have found the following recipe to be adequate:

(1) To 500ml (17.5 liquid ounces) of still base wine, add 25ml (approximately 1 liquid ounce) of brandy or cognac.

(2) With thorough stirring, slowly add table sugar until it no longer goes into solution. The final concentration of sugar should be between 60–70%.

(3) Stopper, and refrigerate for 2–3 weeks before establishing addition levels.

Glossary

*Descriptive Terminology Used in
Wine Evaluation*

This discussion of wine terminologies is centered around the use of the 20-point scale. Within the ten major categories are a miscellany of terms that the enophile may find useful and, in fact, will probably encounter in his or her wine tasting experiences. It should be noted that while a great many more terms could have been included in this presentation, those selected for discussion are the most widely used.

APPEARANCE—Appearance is defined most simply as clarity. Within the category, five subgroupings are generally identified:

(1) Brilliant: a wine of sparkling clarity.
(2) Clear: lacking the sparkling clarity of brilliance, but without visible solids.
(3) Dull: a wine with distinct haze present but usually free of distinct visible solids.
(4) Cloudy: visible solids present.
(5) Turbid: visible solids present in solution as well as precipitate or sediment on sides and bottom of bottle.

A qualifying note is needed in regard to wine clarity. There are increasing numbers of wineries bottling their product as "unfiltered and unfined." In addition, many older wines or imported wines are generally less than brilliant. Unless there are extenuating circumstances (for example, manifest bacterial spoilage), scoring of this category is generally somewhat liberal. It is our experience that with thorough racking the home winemaker should have no trouble in producing a wine that is considered "clear."

COLOR—Each variety has its own range of acceptable color, and experience alone most often dictates the judge's response to this category. The problem is further complicated by the use of generic designations (for example, "Burgundy" or "Chablis") on the label. Generally, the presence of browning overtones in white wines is indicative of oxidation and hence should be scored down. However, in older reds and port wines, loss of "ruby color" is a sign of age and should, therefore, be expected. Thus, color and clarity are good examples of the interdependency of factors involved in any evaluation of wine. This also points out the need for background information on the wine(s) prior to evaluation.

For white wines, color may be divided into four subgroups:

    (1) Nearly colorless or light yellow to light straw. Young wines in this category may or may not have a greenish tint.

    (2) Medium yellow.

(3) Light gold.

(4) Medium gold.

Again, within any variety color may vary depending upon style of winemaking. Increased production from botrytized grapes results in wines that range into the light to medium gold range as compared to group I table wines produced from sound fruit of the same variety.

In the case of red wines, color may vary from pink in Rosé-style wines to light, medium and dark red. Tawney designation is usually restricted to well-aged port wines having a definite brownish coloration. Unfortunately "tawney ports" may also be produced without extensive aging by application of heat or intentional overoxidation.

AROMA and BOUQUET—Use of the term aroma is generally restricted to the odor and character of the unfermented grape. As such, we can refer to the "varietal character," for example, the so-called "green apples character" of Chardonnay and the "raspberry character" of Zinfandel. A wine lacking in varietal personality is often referred to as "vinous."

Bouquet is used in referring to wine after fermentation. Oak aging, for example, contributes to the overall bouquet of the wine. Thus winemakers may refer to "barrel bouquet," or exposure of the wine to the action of oak, and "bottle bouquet," or the marrying of components in a bottled wine.

ACESCENCE—More commonly referred to as volatile acidity or "V.A.," acescence identifies the presence of acetic acid or the vinegar character. Acetic acid, the major volatile acid in wine, is generally recognized as indicative of spoilage. Thus, as its character becomes more pronounced in the wine, available points should be deducted.

TOTAL ACIDITY—As discussed in Chapter 1, acidity of grape wine is primarily the result of tartaric and malic acids respectively. In fruit wines, by comparison, the dominant acid may be malic (in the case of plums, peaches, and the like) or citric (in berries). With respect to acidity, "flat" is used to describe a wine that is deficient in acid, whereas "tart" may be used for well-balanced, high acid wines such as Rieslings. The expression "acidulous" may be applied to objectionably high acid wines produced from green fruit. In cases where acidity overpowers the already deficient or immature character of the variety, points should be deducted.

SUGAR—Although somewhat self-explanatory, sugar identifies not only the presence of the grape sugars, glucose and fructose, but also the "balance" between these and the total wine. If the sweetness level is not compatible with the wine in question, scores should be deducted accordingly. Generally, wines having a reducing sugar level of less than 0.4% are described as "dry." By comparison, "low sugar" or "light sweet" wines range from 0.4% to 5%. "Sweet" designation is applied to wines with more than 5%.

Traditionally, most wines produced are at their best as dry. Current trends, however, are toward increasing production of the light sweet style of white wine. Even the revered Chardonnay grape has been used to a limited extent in production of a sweet style dessert wine. This style of winemaking somewhat complicates the issue of sensory evaluation in that previously established standards (the variety as a dry wine) must be, in part, set aside and the wine evaluated according to modified standards, that is, the variety as a light sweet wine.

BODY—Body is perhaps one of the most difficult and elusive terms for the layman to grasp. This is, in part, because winemakers themselves may disagree as to its definition. Technically defined as the "nonsugar solids present in a wine," body is frequently described in terms of "mouth feel" resulting primarily from its perception as viscosity. In this sense, both alcohol and glycerol are known to increase the viscosity of a wine. Thus, for the purpose of this text, we may guardingly describe body in terms of the alcohol and glycerol content of the wine. As partial support for this, we frequently use glycerol in sensory laboratories for the purpose of demonstrating this sensation.

Body is described as "full," "heavy," or "robust," in the case of intense red wines such as Cabernet Sauvignon or Petite Sirah. The use of "medium" and "light" body is then understood to refer to wines proportionately less intense in this regard.

FLAVOR—As the counterpart to aroma, varietal wines should have a measure of the characteristic flavor(s) of the grape varieties from which they were produced. Wines deficient in this respect are then scored lower. Again, we are dealing with a learning experience; knowledge can only be obtained through firsthand experience with the variety. Thus one should not expect immediate facility with flavor apart from subjective response of approval or disapproval. However, with practice and time, the neophyte will come to recognize even the most subtle of varieties.

In any evaluation of flavor one cannot overlook the contribution of alcohol. Since the alcohol levels for table wines may run from 10-14% (v/v), there is considerable room for "free expression" in winemaking style. However, points should be deducted when the alcoholic taste or "bite" overpowers the other aspects of the wine.

ASTRINGENCY—The result of tannins originating in the grape, astringency is detected as a coarse sensation across the palate, sides and roof of the mouth. Because of skin contact time, red wines have correspondingly more tannin and hence are more astringent than white wines. Upon aging, the tannins in young red wines polymerize and precipitate from solution resulting in a "softening" effect. Wines excessively high in tannin are frequently referred to as being "coarse" or "harsh," the latter being the most undesirable.

Once again, we can point to the importance of qualifying information in fair evaluation of a wine. Obviously, a highly astringent one-year-old Cabernet should be evaluated in a different light from a highly astringent seven-year-old "Cab."

GENERAL QUALITY—As a more or less catch-all category, general quality is the judge's last chance to express himself regarding the overall character of the product. In this category, subtleties that may not have been appropriate to any of the former categories can be expressed. For example, accumulative feelings not significant enough for penalty under the appropriate categories can be deducted here.

With this discussion of score sheet terminology as a groundwork, we can now add to the winemaker's basic vocabulary those expressions that are most frequently used in critiquing a product. Since the majority of terminology that has arisen describes quality defects, these will necessarily receive the emphasis in our discussion. For expedience, these are discussed as to their probable cause.

Several "off odors" may originate from sulfur containing compounds used in either wine processing or as fungicidal agents in the vineyard.

HYDROGEN SULFIDE—Arising primarily from yeast reduction of elemental sulfur present on the grapes at harvest, H_2S is easily discerned as the odor of rotten eggs. Removal of this undesirable volatile component is most easily effected by limited aeration during racking.

MERCAPTANS—Ethyl and methyl mercaptans arise from reaction of ethyl and methyl alcohol and H_2S. Somewhat similar in character to H_2S, mercaptan formation is described as having a "garlic" or "skunky" nose. Since these compounds are difficult to remove once they are formed, prevention is the key. Elimination of H_2S by early and thorough racking is the most effective measure that can be taken to prevent mercaptan formation.

SULFUR DIOXIDE—SO_2, arising from either a recent single addition or as a cumulative effect, produces a burning sensation across the olfactory mucosa as well as on the palate and in the throat. On the palate, SO_2 is reminiscent of peanuts.

Odors from microbial origins are also prevalent in homemade wines and, unfortunately, some commercial products. As discussed under the topic of Wine Microbiology, bacterial involvement, in the case of the malolactic fermentation, may be desirable in certain instances. However, when uncontrolled, spoilage becomes evident in the form of sediment and gas formation, as well as in formation of a variety of malodors. These are discussed briefly in the section that follows.

BACTERIAL—A general term for nondescript spoilage of a microbial nature. In extreme cases, several organisms may have been responsible, producing a variety of metabolic end products such as acetic acid, ethyl acetate, as well as those associated with the malolactic fermentation.

YEASTY—An expression used to describe a wine that has been subject to excessive exposure to yeast either in the form of a very slow fermentation or prolonged contact with lees. Yeasty is sometimes used in describing the undesirable traits of a "lees wine." However, in this case the lees character is the result of a variety of odors of which yeastiness may be of secondary importance.

MOLDY—A mustiness imparted to the wine as a result of contact with mold-contaminated cooperage during aging. Improper storage of empty cooperage is a common problem in the home operation. Under these conditions the inner surfaces of oak barrels support growth from a variety of molds. For a discussion of preventative maintenance consult the appropriate section in Chapter 1.

MOUSEY—Originating during the malolactic fermentation, this character is easily perceived by rubbing a few drops of the wine in question vigorously onto the back of your hand. The odor is not unlike that encountered when cleaning laboratory rodent cages.

LACTIC—As a by-product of the malolactic fermentation, the lactic character is the result of bacterial formation of diacetyl. This compound is described as having a butter-like sensation.

GASSY—A wine with excessive amounts of entrapped carbon dioxide resulting from either a secondary malolactic fermentation or refermentation by yeasts after concentrate addition is termed gassy.

GERANIUM TONE—A geranium-like odor found in sorbic acid stabilized wines that have undergone malo-lactic fermentation. The causative entity is a very volatile ether which is derived from bacterial decomposition of sorbic acid. The expression "geraniol nose" is frequently, and incorrectly, used interchangably to describe the same defect. While geraniol can be isolated from leaf tissue, research has shown that the odor associated with geranium tone problems in wine is bacterial in origin.

ACETIC—Also referred to as acescence, the acetic or vinegar character is the result of oxidative metabolism of wine bacteria of the genus *Acetobacter*.

ALDEHYDIC—A nutty-like character similar to that encountered in sherry, resulting from the activities of the aerobic spoilage yeast *Candida mycoderma* or the sherry yeast *Saccharomyces beticus*. In dessert wines, an aldehydic nose may arise from sources that are nonmicrobial, namely the use of lower quality wine spirits in fortifications.

Obviously, not all defects found in wine can be attributed to the activities of microbes. The following descriptive terminology has its roots in a variety of winery processing operations ranging from receipt of inferior quality grapes to wine spirits additions.

OXIDATION—Resulting from contact of the wine with air, an oxidized wine may be visually detected by browning to one degree or another. Description of the olfactory and gustatory perception of oxidation is difficult, depending upon the variety in question and the extent to which oxidation has occurred. Many winemakers describe oxidation as a loss or decrease in the sharpness or freshness of flavor and aroma components.

RAISINY and STEMMY—Both terms relate to the character of the fruit and nature of the fermentation. Stemmy is used to describe an undesirable woody character resulting from fermentation without adequate separation of stems. The sensation is, in fact, similar to chewing on dried grape stems.

By comparison, raisiny refers to a dried fruit-like character resulting from processing overripe fruit. Both defects are very common in home vinification.

HOT FERMENTATION—Occasionally referred to as "pomacy," the hot fermentation character results from allowing the fermentation to proceed at too high a temperature. In the case of red wines fermented on the skins, a definite pulpy or pomace-like taste and odor may be imparted to the wine.

"Hot" may also be used to describe the use of fortifying alcohol that is high in aldehydes and fusel oils. Both sensations should be distinguished from the "burnt" flavor and odor derived from use of poor quality concentrate to sweeten dry wines. The latter smells and tastes like carmelized sugar.

RUBBERY—As the term implies, a sensation suggestive of old rubber, associated with wines having unusually high pH values.

FILTER PAPER TASTE—Derived from inadequate pretreatment of filtration media, the taste is similar to that detected by chewing on a piece of your filter paper. For home winemakers utilizing filtration, the problem is easily prevented by rinsing filtration media in a mild solution of citric acid followed by neutralization in tap water before use.

We would like to conclude this discussion of the terminology of sensory evaluation on a positive note by mentioning a few terms that winemakers use to praise a product. Expressions such as "clean," "fruity," "well balanced," along with a score of 17 or better, are the winemaker's way of saying "Congratulations! A job well done!"

BILGE—In cooperage, refers to the area of maximum curvature equidistant between the barrel's two heads.

BILGE HOOP—Two hoops closest to the center (bilge) of a barrel.

BUNG—A closure, generally fabricated from redwood, fir, or silicon, used to stopper barrels.

BUNGHOLE—Tapered opening in barrels through which wine is added or withdrawn.

CHAMFER—Refers to sloping stave ends of a barrel.

CHIMES—On a barrel, the portions of the staves between head insert and end.

COOPER—One who manufactures barrels and other wood storage containers.

COOPERAGE—A general term for containers usually constructed of oak, redwood, or chestnut, used for the fermentation and storage of wine and/or brandy. Cooperage also refers to the site at which such containers are fabricated.

CROZE—Groove near the stave ends into which the barrel head is inserted.

HEAD—Refers to the circular ends (top and bottom) of a barrel.

HOOP—General term referring to circular bands of various construction used to hold the barrel staves tightly in place.

HOOP DRIVER—Coopers' tool used to loosen and set hoops.

QUARTER HOOP—Any one of three hoops located

between the head and bilge of a barrel.

SPIKES—Conical wooden dowels used to plug holes in cooperage.

TONNELLERIE—French for cooperage.

WET SURFACE LINER—Food-grade sealant used to *temporarily stop* minor leaks in cooperage.

Appendix I
(A partial listing)

General Wine Supplies

The Compleat Winemaker
   1201 Main Street
   St. Helena, California 94574
   Telephone (707) 963-2400

Wine and the People
   907 University Avenue
   Berkeley, California 94710
   (*Supplies fresh grapes*)

Fresno Home Beer and Wine Making Supplies
   911 E. Belmont Avenue
   Fresno, California 93701

Oak Barrel Winecraft
   1201 University Avenue
   Berkeley, California 94702

Cooperage

Brewers & Bottlers Equipment Corp.
1213 Sixth Avenue
Tampa, Florida 33601

Barrel Builders
1085 Lodi Lane
St. Helena, California 94574

Stefanich Wood Tank Co.
285 W. Shaw Avenue, Suite 204
Fresno, California 93704

Fresh Grapes & Grape Concentrates

Wine and the People
907 University Avenue
Berkeley, California 94710

The Vie Del Company
11903 South Chestnut Avenue
Fresno, California 93721

Analytical Services for Home Winemakers

Bacchus Laboratory
2266 S. De Wolf Ave.
Sanger, California 93657
(209) 441-7153

Metric Conversion Tables

Weights:

1 kilogram (kg)	=	2.2 pounds
1 pound	=	0.454 kilogram
1 kilogram	=	1,000 grams
1 gram	=	0.035 ounces
1 ounce	=	28.3 grams

Volumes:

1 milliliter (ml)	=	0.034 liquid ounces
1 liquid ounce	=	29.5 milliliters
1,000 milliliters	=	1 liter (l)
3.785 liters	=	1 gallon
1 gallon	=	4 quarts
1 quart	=	0.946 liter
1 liter	=	1.057 quarts

References

The following are considered useful supplements to the winemaker's library by the authors.

Books:
Amerine, M. A. and V. L. Singleton, *Introduction to Wine*. Regents of University of California. 2nd Edition revised, 1976.

Amerine, M. A. *Technology of Winemaking*. Avi Publishing Company, 1972.

Amerine, M. A. and M. Joslyn. *Table Wines, the Technology of Their Production*. University of California Press, 1970.

Amerine, M. A. and R. E. Kunkee. *Microbiology of Winemaking*. Ann. Reviews Microbiology 22: 323-358, 1968.

Joslyn, M. and M. A. Amerine. *Dessert, Appetizer and Related Flavored Wines, the technology of their production*. University of California Press, 1964.

Marcus, I. H. *How to Test and Improve Your Wine Judging Ability*. Wine Publications, 1972.

Mitchell, J. R. *Scientific Winemaking Made Easy*. Standard Press Ltd., 1971.

Periodicals:
Wine & Vines. The Hiaring Company, 703 Market Street, San Francisco, California.

Wine World. Wine World Publications, Inc. 15101 Keswick St., Van Nuys, California 91405.

Index

Footnotes

1. *Page 16.* If one wishes to store "wine" active dry yeast between crush periods, or from year to year (which is not recommended), the yeast should be kept in a sealed container, under cool, dry conditions. Since an active yeast culture is essential, it is worthwhile to inquire as to its age. Also, avoid buying yeast packets that have been stored in display windows, as these may have been subject to extremes of temperature.

2. *Page 58:* One of the nicest methods of cooling fermentations of 50 gallons or less is to use plastic citrus juice containers that have been filled with water and frozen. These containers are immersed (with caps firmly tightened!) into the bulk of the fermenting must, as needed, to control temperature increases.

3. *Page 68:* As a concluding remark on fortifications using vodkas, several home winemakers have complained that the volume needed to achieve the desired alcohol level results in too great a dilution. In Nevada one can purchase grain alcohol, at near 190° proof, from retail outlets. Although commercially, winemakers are limited to the use of grape alcohol for fortifications, the home winemaker is not so limited. At this concentration of alcohol, the dilution effect is much smaller.